IC
made easy

Your Key to Understanding Infection Prevention and Control

Joint Commission Resources Mission

The mission of Joint Commission Resources (JCR) is to continuously improve the safety and quality of health care in the United States and in the international community through the provision of education, publications, consultation, and evaluation services.

Disclaimers

JCR educational programs and publications support, but are separate from, the accreditation activities of The Joint Commission. Attendees at Joint Commission Resources educational programs and purchasers of JCR publications receive no special consideration or treatment in, or confidential information about, the accreditation process. The inclusion of an organization name, product, or service in a JCR publication should not be construed as an endorsement of such organization, product, or service, nor is failure to include an organization name, product, or service to be construed as disapproval.

This publication is designed to provide accurate and authoritative information regarding the subject matter covered. Every attempt has been made to ensure accuracy at the time of publication; however, please note that laws, regulations, and standards are subject to change. Please also note that some of the examples in this publication are specific to the laws and regulations of the locality of the facility. The information and examples in this publication are provided with the understanding that the publisher is not engaged in providing medical, legal, or other professional advice. If any such assistance is desired, the services of a competent professional person should be sought.

© 2019 The Joint Commission

Published by Joint Commission Resources
Oak Brook, Illinois 60523 USA
https://www.jcrinc.com/

Joint Commission Resources, Inc. (JCR), a not-for-profit affiliate of The Joint Commission, has been designated by The Joint Commission to publish publications and multimedia products. JCR reproduces and distributes these materials under license from The Joint Commission.

All rights reserved. No part of this publication may be reproduced in any form or by any means without written permission from the publisher. Requests for permission to make copies of any part of this work should be sent to permissions@jcrinc.com.

ISBN (print): 978-1-63585-051-2
ISBN (e-book): 978-1-63585-052-9

Printed in the USA

For more information about The Joint Commission, please visit https://www.jointcommission.org/.

Acknowledgments

Executive Editor: Phyllis Crittenden
Senior Project Manager: Lisa M. King
Associate Director, Publications: Helen M. Fry, MA
Associate Director, Production: Johanna Harris
Executive Director, Global Publishing: Catherine Chopp Hinckley, MA, PhD

Reviewers

Joint Commission Division of of Healthcare Improvement
Sylvia Garcia-Houchins, MBA, RN, CIC, Infection Control Director, Survey Interpretation Group

Joint Commission Resources
Mary Cole, MSN, RN, CIC, CJCP, Domestic Consultant Infection Prevention and Control

Joint Commission International
Barbara Soule, MPA, RN, CIC, FSHEA, IE Consultant, Infection Prevention and Control

Table of Contents

Table of Terms vi

Introduction vii

PART I: Build a Solid Foundation

Chapter 1: Understand the Accreditation Process 1

The Big Idea 1

Key Concepts 1
- Get Ready for the Survey 2
- The SAFER™ Matrix 16

Tool of the Trade 19
- Mock Tracer Form with SAFER™ Matrix

Chapter 2: Prioritize Patient Safety 21

The Big Idea 21

Key Concepts 21
- Responsibility for Infection Prevention and Control 22
- Key Staff and Organizations 23
- Role of Leadership 26
- Build a Team for Infection Prevention and Control 32
- Establish Partnerships 34
- Safely Integrate Technologies 34

Tools of the Trade 37
- Strategies for Engaging Clinicians in IC Activities
- Organizational Assessment for Safety Culture

Chapter 3: Make a Plan and Build a Program 39

The Big Idea 39

Key Concepts 39
- Start Planning 40
- Strategies for Assessing Risk 43
- Establish Goals 48
- Be Prepared 52
- Implement Your Plan 61

Tools of the Trade 73
- Evidence-Based Guidelines Examples for CLABSI Prevention
- Quantitative Risk Assessment Grid
- Injection Safety Checklist

PART II: Comply with Infection Prevention and Control Standards and Goals

Chapter 4: Prevent Transmission of Infections 75
The Big Idea 75
Key Concepts 75
- Use Caution: Prevent Exposure. 76
- Infectious Disease in Health Care Staff 85
- Influenza Vaccinations. 86
- Hand Hygiene Guidelines. 89

Tools of the Trade 93
- Components for Compliance with Joint Commission IC Standards
- Sharps Program Assessment Worksheet
- Strategies for Increasing Influenza Vaccination Rates Among Health Care Workers
- Declination of Influenza (Flu) Vaccination Form

Chapter 5: Prevent Health Care–Associated Infections 95
The Big Idea 95
Key Concepts 95
- Using National Patient Safety Goal 7 as a Guide for Preventing HAIs 96
- Risk Assessment. 101
- Staff Education 103
- Patient and Family Education. 104
- Surveillance. 107
- Implement Evidence-Based Practices 109

Tools of the Trade 110
- Compliance Assessment Checklist for NPSG 7
- Risk Assessment Matrix for Prevention of MDROs
- CDC Checklist for CLABSI Prevention
- Risk Assessment Checklist for Surgical Site Infections

Chapter 6: Provide Safe Medical Equipment, Devices, and Supplies 113
The Big Idea 113
Key Concepts 114
- Categorization of Items to Be Reprocessed Based on Infection Risk. 114
- Common Risks Associated with Cleaning, Disinfection, and Sterilization Failures. 116
- Strategies for Preventing or Mitigating Risk 117

Tools of the Trade 131
- Evaluation of Item for Reprocessing Form
- Steps for Assessing Reprocessing of Instruments, Equipment, and Supplies
- Sample Endoscope Inventory Form

iv

Chapter 7: Manage Infection Prevention and Control in the Environment of Care ... 133

The Big Idea ... 133

Key Concepts ... 134

- Manage Infection Risks in Utility Systems ... 134
- Establish a Safe Environment ... 142
- Assess Infection Risk During Demolition, Renovation, and Construction ... 147

Tools of the Trade ... 150

- Daily Patient Room Cleaning Procedure Checklist
- Environmental Rounds Worksheet for Infection Prevention

Chapter 8: Evaluate and Improve Your Infection Prevention and Control Plan ... 151

The Big Idea ... 151

Key Concepts ... 151

- Evaluate Your Performance ... 152
- Drive Improvement ... 165

Tools of the Trade ... 170

- Performance Improvement Tool Selection Matrix

Index ... 173

Table of Terms

Term	Page	Related Key Concept	Chapter
bioburden	143	Establish a Safe Environment	7
deemed status	25	Key Staff and Organizations	2
evidence-based guidelines	42	Start Planning	3
health care–associated infections	95	Using National Patient Safety Goal 7 as a Guide for Preventing HAIs	5
HEPA filters	141	Manage Infection Risks in Utility Systems	7
Infection control and risk assessment	148	Assess Infection Risk During Demolition, Renovation, and Construction	7
item reprocessing	114	Categorization of Items to Be Reprocessed Based on Infection Risk	6
multidrug-resistant organisms	96	Using National Patient Safety Goal 7 as a Guide for Preventing HAIs	5
patient safety event	32	Role of Leadership	2
performance improvement	165	Drive Improvement	8
personal protective equipment	79	Use Caution: Prevent Exposure	4
risk assessment	41	Start Planning	3
risk assessment	101	Risk Assessment	5
SAFER™ Matrix definitions	17	The SAFER™ Matrix	1
sentinel event	31	Role of Leadership	2
standard precautions	76	Use Caution: Prevent Exposure	4
surveillance	45	Strategies for Assessing Risk	3
tracer	6	Get Ready for the Survey	1

Introduction

Preventing and controlling infection in a health care environment is a big challenge for many organizations. Health care–associated infections can be acquired in any health care setting. Effective strategies to combat the spread of infection are vitally important. If you work in a health care organization, part of your job is to manage infection risks. Everyone is responsible for infection prevention and control (IC), even if you are not the leader of your organization's IC program. This book is designed to help all health care professionals, regardless of their role, to better understand IC. This book aims to make IC easy for you.

This Book Is for You

This book is aimed at four major audiences: accreditation or safety professionals, facilities directors or engineers, clinicians, and leadership at various levels. Although infection preventionists don't need to be introduced to the basics of IC, this book is also a helpful refresher and a resource for IC professionals to share with others in their organization who need to better understand IC.

You're an accreditation or safety professional: You're charged with overseeing overall Joint Commission or Joint Commission International (JCI) standards compliance. You've

got the standards down, but you could use some help navigating the complexities of IC. This book explains complicated IC concepts to better help you deal with safety compliance issues and challenges.

You're a facilities director or engineer: You maintain a safe environment in your organization by assessing potential hazards or risks, evaluating and implementing preventive measures, and ensuring preparation for emergency response plans. This book helps you understand compliance related to IC. It will help your health care organization provide a safe environment for patients and staff, free from infection.

You're a clinician: You are a caregiver in a health care organization. You work directly in providing patient care, treatment, and service as a nurse, care technician, physician, or other direct caregiver. This book will help to better acquaint you with possible infection risks, the dangers to staff and patients, and how to prevent them.

You're in a leadership position: Your job is to understand how your staff can mitigate infection and provide the resources needed to prevent it. You need to know how to handle the myriad dangers of infection, how it can affect staff and patients, and what to do to control it. This book gives you the background to prepare for and understand conversations with your infection preventionists, facilities staff, and accreditation professionals. It will give you confidence in the decisions you need to make regarding IC protocols.

You're working together: In a health care organization, you never work alone. You are a team. This book is designed to help all of you to better communicate and collaborate for IC.

- **Infection preventionist:** You're THE expert in your organization for IC. You are responsible for your organization's policies and procedures regarding infection and ensuring that those policies and procedures are followed properly. You know your stuff but would love an easy-to-use reference or a resource to share with others.

Introduction

- **Accreditation professionals:** You have to know a lot about a lot of different areas of your health care organization. IC is a big one. Maybe you aren't familiar with all the latest IC guidelines, but you are still responsible for ensuring that your organization is in compliance with Joint Commission standards and best practices. You can go over concepts in this book to enhance your understanding. It's also nice to use this book to translate IC concepts to clinicians and leadership.
- **Facilities directors:** You can use this book to help better identify and manage risks related to infection and the physical environment, get up to speed and/or update your knowledge of IC concepts, and then be able to communicate with others on the health care team, including accreditation professionals and leadership.
- **Leaders:** You can use the book to prime yourself for any and all discussions of IC with accreditation, clinical, or facilities staff. You know that IC is a priority, and you need to know and understand the lingo and the concepts. This book will help you do that.

The Joint Commission

The Joint Commission accredits and certifies more than 21,000 health care organizations and programs in the United States. Joint Commission accreditation and certification is recognized nationwide as a symbol of quality that reflects your organization's commitment to meeting certain performance standards. Infection prevention and control comprises a significant portion of Joint Commission standards and National Patient Safety Goals

Joint Commission Resources

Joint Commission International (JCI) identifies, measures, and shares best practices in quality and patient safety with the world. JCI has accredited more than 1,000 health care organizations around the world. We provide leadership and innovative solutions to help health care organizations across all settings improve performance and outcomes. Our expert team works with hospitals and other health care organizations, health systems, government ministries, public health agencies, academic institutions, and businesses to achieve peak performance in patient care. Infection prevention and control is a key area of JCI requirements for health care organizations.

This Book Is for All Settings

Whether you are addressing infections in a hospital operating room, laboratory, outpatient facility, or residential health facility, this book will present Joint Commission standards and solutions related to IC in your area of specialty, although some differences do exist in these various care settings. This book also discusses JCI requirements and compliance solutions for health care organizations around the globe.

This Book Focuses on the Basics

No matter what your job is or in what setting you perform that job, you will benefit from a guide to IC that's easy to understand and reference. This book is it. Below is an introduction to the basic concepts of IC in health care organizations, how to identify problems, and how to implement strategies to prevent infection in the first place.

Standards related to IC appear in the Joint Commission accreditation manual chapter "Infection Prevention and Control" (IC) and the Joint Commission International accreditation manual chapter "Prevention and Control of Infections" (PCI).

Basic elements: IC is made up of three basic elements to mitigate risk:
- **Planning:** This includes responsibility, resources, risks, and goals needed to prevent infection.
- **Implementation:** This includes medical equipment, devices, supplies, and vaccinations that support patient care in your facility, as well as the human actions necessary to prevent the transmission of infections.
- **Evaluation and Improvement:** This includes the important steps for a health care organization to sustain its efforts to control and prevent infection.

Basic risk areas and manual chapters: Joint Commission and JCI accreditation standards are designed to address risks. IC is such an important activity that both Joint Commission and JCI have dedicated an entire chapter of accreditation requirements related to the topic.

Introduction

- Safety: This area addresses risks usually related to accidental incidents that occur during everyday tasks, in the physical structure, or due to uncontrollable factors. It also includes worker safety and maintaining a healthy environment, one that is infection free.
- Hazardous materials and waste: To be compliant, you have to manage hazardous materials and waste from the time they enter the facility to the time they leave it. This area is all about managing the many risks involved in all the processes for handling these materials.
- Medical equipment: This area addresses risks related to equipment used in monitoring, treatment, diagnosis, or direct care of patients. Inventory, inspection, testing, and maintenance are primary activities involved in managing these risks.

Book Organization and Format

This book is organized in a way that makes it easy to find the information you need quickly. All content is clearly labeled and consistently formatted, with core and extra features distinguished for targeted reading.

Parts of the book: The book is organized into two parts:

Part I: Build a Solid Foundation
- Chapter 1: Understand the Accreditation Process
- Chapter 2: Prioritize Patient Safety
- Chapter 3: Make a Plan and Build a Program

Part II: Comply with Infection Prevention and Control Standards and Goals
- Chapter 4: Prevent Transmission of Infections
- Chapter 5: Prevent Health Care–Associated Infections
- Chapter 6: Provide Safe Medical Equipment, Devices, and Supplies
- Chapter 7: Manage Infection Prevention and Control in the Environment of Care
- Chapter 8: Evaluate and Improve Your Infection Prevention and Control Plan

Chapter features: Each chapter includes the same types of features presented in the same order, so navigation is easy. And in the e-book version, internal links allow you to easily search for terms and navigate across chapters. Links even take you directly to the downloadable, customizable tools (in the print version, these tools are provided online*).

This chart shows the chapter features in this book. Some features appear in the margins to correspond to the core content.

Chapter Feature	Purpose of Feature
The Big Idea	Presents the overall chapter topic/provides an overview.
Key Concepts	Highlights core ideas.
In Other Words	Defines key terms in plain language. No jargon!
Try This Tool	Lists downloadable, customizable tools and how they can be used.
Smart Questions	Asks questions to begin focused discussion on infection prevention and control topics.
Picture THIS	Highlights important topics and concepts visually.

Acknowledgments

Joint Commission Resources gratefully acknowledges the time and insights of the subject matter experts at The Joint Commission and Joint Commission International. We would also like to thank our writer, Markisan Naso.

---

* Print edition: Go to https://www.jcrinc.com/assets/1/7/ICME18_Try_This_Tool.pdf and click on the download links.

PART I: Build a Solid Foundation

CHAPTER 1

Understand the Accreditation Process

The Joint Commission and Joint Commission International (JCI) accredit health care organizations that meet requirements or standards related to high-quality, safe patient care. But more than that, the accreditation process is designed to inspire your health care organization to continuously improve its care, treatment, and services for patients. The accreditation process includes a thorough evaluation of your facility during an on-site survey that features facility tours, staff discussions and observations, and tracers.

KEY CONCEPTS

- Get Ready for the Survey
- The SAFER™ Matrix

KEY CONCEPT

Get Ready for the Survey

If you're reading this book, you're interested in bolstering patient safety and quality of care at your facility. That is the focus of the Joint Commission accreditation process. The process starts with observation and assessment of standards compliance in the form of surveys. Among other activities, the survey includes an evaluation of the health care organization's compliance with The Joint Commission's Infection Prevention and Control (IC) standards or JCI's Prevention and Control of Infections (PCI) standards, as well as National Patient Safety Goals (NPSGs) or International Patient Safety Goals (IPSGs) related to IC. (*See* the box on page 3.)

The Joint Commission Survey Process

To determine how your organization can improve, The Joint Commission evaluates a meaningful assessment of your patient care and organizational processes to help you identify safety risks. (This section refers to the US survey process; *see* a discussion of the JCI Survey Process on page 7.) The surveyor's objective is to help health care organizations improve quality and safety through compliance with Joint Commission or JCI standards. They accomplish this by observing processes, taking notes, reviewing documents, conducting tracers, asking questions, and objectively evaluating compliance. Joint Commission surveyors are there to help you learn and improve at your organization. They will provide feedback to your organization, create reports, and discuss strategies to help fix any problems they discover. (*See* Figure 1-1 for a sample Joint Commission survey agenda.)

What type of survey can I expect? Surveys are designed to be individualized to each organization. The length of the survey depends on the organization's size, complexity, and scope of services. After submitting your electronic application for accreditation (E-App), The Joint Commission or JCI will work with you to schedule an initial survey. Joint Commission surveys for reaccreditation are unannounced, whereas JCI surveys are scheduled with the organization. A complete discussion of the survey process and eligibility can be found in "The Accreditation

Chapter 1 | **Understand the Accreditation Process**

Infection Prevention
and Control Requirements

The Joint Commission addresses IC in the "Infection Prevention and Control" standards chapter, found in the *Comprehensive Accreditation Manual* or E-dition. National Patient Safety Goal 7 also addresses IC issues. Joint Commission International (JCI) addresses IC in its "Prevention and Control of Infections" (PCI) chapter, as well as in International Patient Safety Goal 5.

The IC and PCI Standards

The processes outlined in the IC (Joint Commission) and PCI (JCI) chapters are applicable to all infections or potential sources of infection that a health care organization might encounter, including a sudden influx of potentially infectious patients. The standards are designed to assist organizations, both large and small, in developing and maintaining an effective program that covers a wide range of situations.

These standards address activities of planning, implementation, and evaluation and are based on the following conditions necessary to establish and operate an effective IC program:

- Recognize that its IC program plays a major role in its efforts to improve patient safety and quality of care.
- Demonstrate leadership's commitment to IC by endorsing and participating in the organization's efforts to control infection, provide resources, and encourage improvement.
- See that staff collaborate with each other when designing and implementing the IC program.

- Regularly assess its IC program by using an epidemiological approach that consists of surveillance, data collection, analysis, and trend identification. Coordinate its IC program with the larger community.
- Take into account that the potential exists for an infection outbreak so extensive that it overwhelms the organization's resources.

National Patient Safety Goal 7

In 2002 The Joint Commission established its National Patient Safety Goals (NPSGs) program; the first set of goals became effective January 1, 2003. The goals were established to help accredited organizations address specific areas of concern in regards to patient safety.

Goal 7 requires organizations to reduce the risk of health care–associated infections (HAIs). Requirements include the following:

- Meeting hand hygiene guidelines (NPSG.07.01.01)
- Preventing multidrug-resistant organism infections (NPSG.07.03.01)
- Preventing central line–associated bloodstream infections (NPSG.07.04.01)

- Preventing surgical site infections (NPSG.07.05.01)
- Preventing catheter-associated urinary tract infections (NPSG.07.06.01)

International Patient Safety Goal 5

Similar to the National Patient Safety Goal, International Patient Safety Goal (IPSG) 5 requires JCI–accredited organizations to reduce the risk of HAIs. Associated with this goal is requirement IPSG.5: The organization adopts and implements evidence-based hand hygiene guidelines to reduce the risk of HAIs.

Figure 1-1 Sample Survey Agenda

Survey Activity Name	Suggested Duration of Activity	Suggested Scheduling of Activity	Organization Participants (Refer to Survey Activity Guide for more info.)
Surveyor Arrival and Preliminary Planning	30-60 minutes	1st day, upon arrival	
Opening Conference and Orientation to the Organization	30-60 minutes	1st day, as early as possible	
Surveyor Planning Initial	30-60 minutes	1st day, as early as possible	
Individual Tracer	60-120 minutes	Individual tracer activity occurs each day throughout the survey; the number of individuals that surveyors trace varies by organization. If travel is required to perform tracer activity (e.g., to an outpatient setting), it will be planned into this time.	
Lunch	30 minutes	At a time negotiated with the organization	
Issue Resolution	30 minutes	End of each day except last; can be scheduled at other times as necessary	
Team Meeting/Surveyor Planning	30 minutes	Mid-day and/or end of each day except first and last	
Daily Briefing	30-45 minutes	Start of each survey day except the first day; can be scheduled at other times as necessary	
Competence Assessment	30-60 minutes	After some individual tracer activity has occurred; at a time negotiated with the organization	
Medical Staff Credentialing & Privileging	60 minutes	After some individual tracer activity has occurred; at a time negotiated with the organization	
Environment of Care	60-90 minutes	After some individual tracer activity has occurred; at a time negotiated with the organization	
Emergency Management	60-90 minutes	After some individual tracer activity has occurred; at a time negotiated with the organization	
System Tracer – Data Management	60-90 minutes	After some individual tracer activity has occurred; at a time negotiated with the organization. If this is the only system tracer taking place during survey, the topics of Infection Control and Medication Management will be covered in this discussion.	
Leadership	60 minutes	Toward the middle or end of survey at a time negotiated with the organization	
Report Preparation	60-120 minutes	Last day of survey	
CEO Exit Briefing	15-30 minutes	Last day of survey	
Organization Exit Conference	30-45 minutes	Last day, final activity of survey	
Note: The following activities may be incorporated into the survey agenda as noted under the Suggested Scheduling of Activity column.			
System Tracer – Infection Control	60 minutes	Occurs on surveys greater than three days in duration. After some individual tracer activity has	

Chapter 1 | Understand the Accreditation Process

Figure 1-1 Sample Survey Agenda *continued*

Survey Activity Name	Suggested Duration of Activity	Suggested Scheduling of Activity	Organization Participants (Refer to Survey Activity Guide for more info.)
		occurred; at a time negotiated with the organization.	
System Tracer – Medication Management	60 minutes	Occurs on surveys greater than three days in duration. After some individual tracer activity has occurred; at a time negotiated with the organization.	
Interim Exit – w/ early departing surveyors & organization	30 minutes	At the end of any day another program surveyor or life safety code specialist is departing from the survey in advance of the team	
Life Safety Code® Survey Activity			
Life Safety Code Specialist Arrival and Preliminary Planning Session	30 minutes	LSCS survey 1st day, early	
Facility Orientation/ Maintenance Document Review	60-90 minutes	At a time negotiated with the organization	
Life Safety Code® Building Assessment	2-5 hours per day	At a time negotiated with the organization	
Lunch	30 minutes	At a time negotiated with the organization	
Facility Maintenance / Document Review (Critical Access Hospital ONLY)	60-90 minutes	At a time negotiated with the organization	
Environment of Care & Emergency Management (Critical Access Hospital ONLY)	60-90 minutes	At a time negotiated with the organization	
Facility Tracer / Issue resolution (Critical Access Hospital ONLY)	30 minutes	At a time negotiated with the organization	
Report Preparation	60 minutes	Toward the end of last day of survey	
Interim Exit	30 minutes	Last activity on last day of survey	

Process" (ACC) chapter of your *Comprehensive Accreditation Manual* or E-dition, or the "Summary of Key Accreditation Policies" in the JCI manual.

How often do surveys occur? In general, every accredited organization must be surveyed between 18 and 36 months after the last completed survey. However, if your organization is accredited under the Laboratory and Point-of-Care Testing Accreditation Program, your survey will occur within 24 months. A survey can be conducted at any moment within the time frame, so your organization must maintain continuous compliance and be prepared for a surveyor visit.

Tracer Methodology

Tracer methodology is the key survey assessment method used by Joint Commission and JCI surveyors. Its purpose is to assess your health care organization's compliance with Joint Commission or JCI accreditation and certification standards. It involves tracking (or "tracing") patients' experiences through the continuum of care within a health care organization.

Why conduct tracers? By studying the complex systems of your health care organization, surveyors can identify system deficiencies and then help your organization correct them so they don't harm patients or staff. There are multiple forms of tracers, but they all seek to achieve the following three goals:

1. An integrated and cross-sectional review of areas most critical to safe, high-quality care (for example, intensive care units, operating rooms)
2. A focused analysis of compliance with standards (for example, IC standards)
3. Specific information about the organization that can be used to design and target improvements (for example, review of disinfection and sterilization)

- **Evaluation and assistance:** A tracer also allows a surveyor to provide guidance to your organization and staff by evaluating your systems and performance. Such evaluation will assist your organization with the following:

in other words

Tracer

A tracer is a process used by surveyors to analyze an organization's systems by following or "tracing" an individual patient through the care, treatment, and services process.

Chapter 1 | **Understand the Accreditation Process**

The Joint Commission International Survey Process

An accreditation survey is designed to assess an organization's compliance with Joint Commission International (JCI) standards based on the following:

- Interviews with staff and patients and other verbal information
- On-site observations of patient care processes
- Review of policies, procedures, clinical practice guidelines, medical records, staff records, governmental and/or regulatory compliance reports, and other documents requested from the organization
- Review of quality and patient safety improvement data, performance measures, and outcomes
- Individual patient tracers (that is, evaluation of a patient's care experience through the care process)
- System tracers of organizationwide processes (for example, medication management, infection control, hazardous waste and materials, or other high-risk, high/low-volume, problem-prone systems and processes).

JCI and the health care organization select the survey date and prepare the survey agenda together to meet the organization's needs and the requirements for an efficient survey.

Planning the Survey Agenda

Each organization is assigned a team leader to assist in the coordination of the survey agenda planning. The team leader will contact the organization approximately eight weeks in advance of the survey to coordinate logistics for the on-site survey and prepare a survey agenda based on the size, type, and complexity of the organization. The agenda specifies the sites surveyors will visit, the types of interviews surveyors will conduct, the staff to be interviewed, and the documents that must be provided to the surveyors.

Survey Process

Tracer methodology is the foundation of the on-site survey process. In the tracer methodology, surveyors select representative patients from the organization's patient population and trace each patient's care experience; they will also trace several key clinical and managerial systems processes.

This methodology allows surveyors to identify standards compliance issues evident in one or more steps of the patient care and management processes or in the interfaces between processes.

In addition, surveyors interview staff individually and in groups, observe patient care, speak to patients and their families, review patient medical records, review staff personnel records, and review policies and procedures and other documents.

The surveyors confer with the organization's chief executive officer and other leaders at a leadership conference at the end of each survey. During this conference, the surveyors provide preliminary information about their findings. It is important to note that any preliminary information is not final until the review by JCI Accreditation Central Office staff has been completed.

If, during the survey, the surveyors identify any condition they believe poses a serious threat to public or patient safety, they notify the JCI Accreditation Central Office staff. In those circumstances, JCI decides whether to issue an expedited Denial of Accreditation decision and if it should inform relevant public authorities.

7

- **Risks:** Identifying areas of concern or risk related to the physical environment and IC
- **Strengths:** Identifying organization strengths in preventing/mitigating risk related to the physical environment and IC
- **Compliance:** Assessing adherence to Joint Commission requirements
- **Actions/Interventions:** Determining actions necessary for addressing areas of concern

Individual tracer: An individual tracer is a tool that surveyors use to follow or "trace" a single patient through his or her process of care. Surveyors observe a patient, talk to staff and the patient about the care he or she receives, and review the system processes. The idea is to focus on the experience of the patient and look for how well your organization provides for his or her needs and safety. For example, the individual tracer may follow a patient admitted through the emergency department and identified as having a communicable disease or a multi-drug-resistant organism or be on antibiotics.

System tracer: System tracers are additional, interactive sessions that allow a surveyor to perform a more detailed exploration of a particular area, process, or subject, evaluating the performance of important patient-related functions that cross the organization. The three topics currently evaluated by system tracers are data management, infection control, and medication management. As you can see, The Joint Commission believes that IC is a vital system of a health care organization that needs to be carefully assessed and analyzed via a system tracer. No wonder we're doing a book on this topic!

IC system tracer
One example of a system tracer may involve IC or PCI processes. These tracers assess the organization's practices to ensure compliance with relevant Joint Commission or JCI standards. The tracer is designed to identify related issues and identify actions that can improve patient safety.

This helps surveyors determine the strengths and vulnerabilities of your organization's IC plan and its implementation. Within this type of tracer, the surveyor will ask questions related to infection

Chapter 1 | **Understand the Accreditation Process**

risks in the physical environment, as well as other aspects of IC. Consider the following examples:

- What are the highest priorities identified on the IC risk assessment? What are the plans to address these priorities?
- What do the IC surveillance data show as problem areas for device-related infections such as central lines and urinary catheters?
- What are the organization's strategies to reduce the risk of infections associated with medical equipment, devices, and supplies?
- How would the organization manage infection risks if utilities were not available; for example, how would hand hygiene be performed without a water source?
- How does the organization work to prevent the transmission of infectious diseases, including those caused by waterborne and airborne pathogens?

Sample Tracer Scenario: Infection Control System Tracer in an Office-Based Surgery Practice

This infection control system tracer was conducted at an office-based surgery (OBS) practice located in a suburban community in the United States. The OBS practice is a small organization with eight staff members, including three physicians. It opened eight years earlier and provides endoscopies and colonoscopies. During the on-site survey, the surveyor conducted an infection control system tracer in which she examined the organization's infection prevention and control (IC) systems. She spoke with various staff in the practice, including the medical director, one of the operative nurses, and the nursing manager who has oversight responsibility for IC. The bracketed numbers throughout the scenario correspond to questions the surveyor could ask during a tracer.

The surveyor first wanted to explore how the practice has established and monitors its IC activities and who is involved in carrying out the work and overseeing it. [1, 2] The team explained that all staff are involved but that the primary responsibility rests with the practice's nurse manager, who also has responsibility for documenting the IC work and various activities. The surveyor also learned that the nurse manager is responsible for providing new and ongoing staff orientation to IC activities in the practice. [3, 4] The surveyor also wanted to understand how the practice follows hand hygiene guidelines and how patients are informed about

9

them. [5] The surveyor then asked to review the organization's approach to handling and cleaning its equipment, particularly between procedures in the practice and when the practice is extremely busy; she also wanted to know what kinds of guidelines the practice follows. [6]

The surveyor then asked staff to explain how they identify, manage, and document risks in the practice. [7, 8] She examined documents related to the organization's risk assessment and found that risks were identified, but they were not prioritized or clearly communicated to staff. The surveyor also found, when exploring staff vaccination practices, that although the organization had implemented a program to vaccinate staff against influenza, improving vaccination rates was not included as a goal in its written IC plan. [9]

At the end of the survey, the surveyor and staff discussed improving processes for ensuring that the goal to improve vaccination rates is written into the practice's own plan and that measures are put in place to determine progress achieved within a set period.

Sample Questions
The following represent some questions that could be asked during a tracer. Use them as a starting point to plan your own tracers.

1. Who is responsible for carrying out the work of infection prevention and control and who oversees it?
2. How do you monitor the effectiveness of your program? How is this documented?
3. What are your surgical site infection rates and how do you monitor these?
4. How do you educate staff about the infection prevention and control systems and risk-reduction activities in the practice?
5. What is your approach to hand hygiene guidelines? How are staff educated about them?
6. How do you handle cleaning, sterilizing, or sanitizing equipment, devices, or supplies used within the practice? What guidelines do you follow?
7. How do you identify risks in the practice?
8. What risk-reduction activities do you have in place for preventing surgical site infections? How are these documented and communicated with staff?
9. How are staff engaged with specific infection prevention and control activities that directly affect their safety, such as vaccinations, prevention of sharps injuries, and appropriate use of personal protective equipment?

Chapter 1 | **Understand the Accreditation Process**

Role of staff in tracer methodology: To help a surveyor in the tracer methodology process, staff at your organization will be asked to provide a list of active patients. This includes the patients' names, current locations in the health care organization, and diagnoses or conditions. The surveyor may also request assistance from staff to select tracer patients.

As the surveyor moves around your facility, expect him or her to speak with staff members involved in the tracer patient's care, treatment, or services. If they aren't available, the surveyor will talk to another staff member who performs the same duties.

Discussion topics: During a system tracer, the surveyor will engage relevant staff in an interactive session. Points of discussion in the interactive session may include the following:

- The flow of the process across the health care organization, including identification and management of risk points, integration of key activities, and communication among staff or units involved in the process
- Strengths in the process and possible actions to be taken in areas needing improvement
- Issues requiring further exploration in other survey activities
- A baseline assessment of standards compliance
- Education by the surveyor, as appropriate

Sample Tracer Scenario: Influx of Infectious Patients in a Major Metropolitan Area

This tracer was conducted across four hospitals in the same system, each facility located in a major metropolitan area. During the tracer, the surveyor examined the system's level of preparedness for an influx of potentially infectious patients. The surveyor met with infection preventionists, patient safety staff, and members of the emergency management and planning team at each hospital, as well as systemwide coordinators. The bracketed numbers throughout the scenario correspond to questions the surveyor could ask during a tracer.

The surveyor first asked staff to describe what their emergency plans were across the system, particularly in relation to the types of emergencies they were planning for and the policies and procedures they had in place. [1, 2] He also wanted to know what

their overall communication plan was in the event of an emergency and what training and testing they undertook in consideration of each contingency. [3, 4, 5]

Staff members shared their emergency planning approach, which was standardized across the system, though the specifics of each hospital's plan included customized material suitable to risks in its local area.

Considering each hospital's plan, the surveyor noticed a lack of detail in the system's plans for an infectious outbreak. The system had a strong internal communication plan, but hospitals needed to bolster communication with community response agencies, as well as with the hospitals' suppliers. Staff education, system testing, and training were also well documented in the plan, but implementation of some of these programs was delayed at two of the hospitals.

The surveyor learned that each hospital had a shared written plan for responding to such an influx. [6] The surveyor wanted to understand each plan's level of specificity, and he found that each hospital's plan was not adequately shaped around the needs of that hospital's specific patient population, including consideration for varying socioeconomic and health needs. [7]

The surveyor also wanted to know how the system addressed staff training, as well as how the system stayed on top of clinical and epidemiological information regarding new infection risks. [8, 9] Regular training was well documented at each hospital, but one hospital's approach to collecting and sharing information appeared inconsistent.

To improve planning, the surveyor and team discussed reviewing and updating the existing plans and processes to ensure that all hospitals were following a process that suited their own setting and population served.

Sample Questions
The following represent some questions that could be asked during a tracer. Use them as a starting point to plan your own tracers.

1. Please describe your system's approach to emergency planning. What specific plans do you have at each hospital?
2. What are your policies and procedures for emergency planning? How are they reviewed and updated? Who has responsibility for the policies and procedures?
3. Please describe your communication plan for emergencies. What happens in the event of an influx of infectious patients?

Chapter 1 | **Understand the Accreditation Process**

4. When communicating information about an emergency, who is on your call tree? How does this function at both the system and local hospital level? What about agencies beyond the hospital and system?
5. What training and testing do you undertake in relation to emergency planning? How often does this take place and how is it documented?
6. What is your approach to planning for an influx of infectious patients? How is this documented?
7. What determines your specific approach to planning for an influx at each hospital? How do you factor in demographics and the patient cohort's health needs?
8. How are staff trained on emergency procedures, particularly in relation to testing processes, equipment, and responses? How are they trained on responding to an influx of infectious patients, for example?
9. How do you stay on top of current clinical and epidemiological information about infections?

Discussion participants: Participants may include the infection preventionist, nurses, physicians, laboratorians, the environmental services director, coordinators of safety or quality management activities, the risk manager, an accreditation professional at your organization, the facilities director, and other individuals responsible for management of IC or patient safety (safety, security, hazardous materials and waste, medical equipment, and utilities). Of course, who is involved depends on what type of health care organization you are. Not every type of health care organization has separate people fulfilling each role; in smaller or other types of health care organizations, one or two individuals may wear multiple hats.

A surveyor will talk through any potential vulnerabilities related to the issues flagged in a tracer. Organizational and staff response to these risks, along with potential solutions will also be discussed.

COLLABORATION: Accreditation surveys are a collaborative process. Your post-survey follow-up should also be collaborative. If you're a facilities director or accreditation professional or infection preventionist in a recently surveyed organization, invite

> ## Perform Your Own Tracer
>
> **Mock tracer:** You can conduct your own simulation, or mock tracer, based on actual Joint Commission tracers.
>
> **Why conduct mock tracers?** The information gathered from a tracer is used to uncover opportunities for improvement in your organization. But you don't have to wait until your facility is officially surveyed to get this information. Organizations can conduct their own mock tracers as a part of their performance improvement activities. This helps the organization do the following:
> - Engage staff and leadership in accreditation activities, such as regular assessment of compliance with standards.
> - Identify deficiencies to later address them with interventions and sustain improvements.
> - Prepare for your next on-site survey.
> - Increase confidence in the survey process.

clinicians, leaders, and staff to meet to talk about their survey experiences. Discuss the positive aspects of the survey and request suggestions for improvement. Consider creating survey readiness activities, soliciting volunteers or the IC Committee to participate and build a mock tracer program that specifically addresses IC.

Documentation

Joint Commission and JCI surveyors will request information and documentation on-site. You should provide them with whatever documentation they request. This information is evaluated and used throughout the survey as reference, as well as to develop tracers.

Surveyors performing IC surveys require documentation for the following:
- Policies governing control of infections and communicable diseases
- Policies governing control of infections and communicable diseases.
- The organization's system for identifying, reporting, investigating, and controlling health care–associated infections and communicable diseases
- Risk assessment and prioritizing risks for acquiring and transmitting infections
- Outbreak investigation (international)

smart questions:

How does your organization account for all required written documentation required by The Joint Commission or JCI? Is this documentation kept readily available?

Chapter 1 | **Understand the Accreditation Process**

- Written IC goals for your organization, such as the following examples:
  - Addressing its prioritized risks
  - Limiting unprotected exposure to pathogens
  - Limiting the transmission of infections associated with procedures
  - Limiting the transmission of infections associated with the use of medical equipment, devices, and supplies
  - Improving compliance with hand hygiene guidelines
  - Education for IC
  - Integration of IC with quality and patient safety
- A written description of the activities of your organization's IC plan, including surveillance, to minimize, reduce, or eliminate the risk of infection
- A written process for how your organization will investigate outbreaks of infectious disease
- A written process for how your organization will respond to an influx of potentially infectious patients
- Incremental influenza vaccination goals, consistent with achieving the 90% rate established in the national influenza initiatives for 2020 (particularly for organizations in the United States)
- A written description of your organization's methodology used to determine influenza vaccination rates
- A record of your organization improving its vaccination rates according to its established goals at least annually
- Evidence that the IC program is based on scientific knowledge, practice guidelines, applicable laws and regulations, and standards for sanitation and cleanliness (this is international)
- Evidence that the hospital leadership provides resources to support the IC (PCI) program

Other required written documentation:
- Additional documents may be requested as well. Documentation identified in a standard or element of performance (EP) or the measurable element (ME) labeled with the Ⓓ icon should be provided to surveyors on request during any part of the survey. You can refer to the "Required Written Documentation" (RWD) chapter in your accreditation manual or try using

smart questions:

Do you have an infection control committee or other coordination mechanism such as a quality or patient safety committee that can discuss a survey after it's completed?

the documentation filter available in the E-dition. There is also a general list in the *Accreditation Survey Activity Guide for Health Care Organizations*, which is kept updated on your organization's Joint Commission Connect™ extranet site, or *JCI Direct Connect* for organizations outside the United States.

KEY CONCEPT
The SAFER™ Matrix

The survey process is all about identifying and communicating risk levels associated with deficiencies so they can be minimized or eliminated. To help organizations prioritize and focus their corrective actions, The Joint Commission created the Survey Analysis for Evaluating Risk™ (SAFER™) Matrix. This scoring tool gives surveyors the ability to perform real-time, on-site evaluations of deficiencies. It also allows your organization to better classify different risk levels posed by noncompliance with standards. (JCI does not currently use the SAFER Matrix.)

How the SAFER Matrix process works: Each standard has associated EPs, which are the performance expectations for determining if your organization is in compliance with a standard. If your organization is found to be out of compliance, the noncompliant EP will be cited as a Requirement for Improvement (RFI) and placed in the SAFER Matrix. Each RFI observation recorded by a surveyor is then plotted on the SAFER Matrix according to the likelihood that the issue will cause harm to patients, staff, or visitors (low, moderate, high), as well as the scope of the problem (limited, pattern, widespread).

The idea is to help your organization focus its improvement efforts. RFIs placed in the upper right regions (dark orange or red boxes) of the matrix pose a greater risk in terms of the number of persons potentially affected or the severity of that risk.

Any observations of noncompliance are documented in the SAFER Matrix and require follow-up activity based on surveyors' observations. A time frame of 60 days is allotted for corrective action.

TRY THIS TOOL

Mock Tracer Form with SAFER™ Matrix

Use this tool to conduct mock tracers in your organization. It includes the SAFER matrix, which helps identify compliance issues and focus your attention on areas that need improvement.

16

Chapter 1 | **Understand the Accreditation Process**

IC issues in the SAFER Matrix: IC findings are placed in the SAFER Matrix according to their likelihood of harm, just like any other identified deficiencies. You can try using the SAFER Matrix in your own performance improvement initiatives. Apply the same criteria of likelihood of harm and scope to the risk issues you encounter daily. This will be useful as you develop your risk assessment, IC plan, and compliance strategies.

See "The SAFER Matrix" Picture This feature on page 18 for information to help your organization better understand the SAFER Matrix process. For more information or questions about the SAFER Matrix, *see* the webinar replay and slides on the Joint Commission website.

Immediate Threat to Health or Safety

An Immediate Threat to Health or Safety," also known as "Immediate Threat to Life" (ITL), is plotted on the SAFER Matrix in the top row. An ITL is a situation that may potentially have serious adverse effects on the health of a patient, resident, or individual. Any discovered ITL must be corrected immediately. For example, improperly sterilized or high-level disinfected (HLD) equipment could be considered an ITL. During 2016, 74% of all ITL declarations from The Joint Commission were related to improperly sterilized or HLD equipment.

Continuous Compliance

The Joint Commission and JCI expect an accredited organization to be in continuous compliance with all requirements. In other words, it's important to maintain a consistently high level of safety and care at all times. This includes the standards related to IC. The following outline lists topics addressed by the standards discussed in detail throughout this book.

Joint Commission IC Standards
- I. Planning
  - A. Responsibility (IC.01.01.01)
  - B. Resources (IC.01.02.01)
  - C. Risks (IC.01.03.01)
  - D. Goals (IC.01.04.01)
  - E. Activities (IC.01.05.01)
  - F. Influx (IC.01.06.01)

in other words

SAFER Matrix definitions

Each Requirement for Improvement (RFI) recorded by a surveyor is plotted on the SAFER Matrix according to the likelihood that the issue will cause harm to patients, staff, or visitors, as well as the scope of the problem. The levels of harm and scope are defined as follows:

Harm

- **High:** Occurrence of harm is likely. In other words, the finding could directly lead to harm without need for other significant circumstances or failures.
- **Moderate:** Occurrence of harm is possible. In other words, the finding could cause harm directly but is more likely to cause harm as a contributing factor.
- **Low:** Occurrence of harm is rare. In other words, the finding undermines safety or contributes to an unsafe environment.

Scope

- **Limited:** A unique occurrence that doesn't happen routinely. It has the potential to affect only a limited number of patients, visitors, or staff.
- **Pattern:** Multiple occurrences of the RFI, or a single occurrence that has the potential to affect more than a limited number of patients, visitors, or staff.
- **Widespread:** Deficiency is pervasive in the facility, represents systemic failure, or has the potential to affect most or all patients, visitors, and staff.

The SAFER Matrix

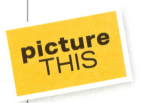

Likelihood to Harm a Patient/Staff/Visitor

	LIMITED	PATTERN	WIDESPREAD
HIGH			
MODERATE			
LOW			

Immediate Threat to Life (a threat that represents immediate risk or may potentially have serious adverse effects on the health of the patient, resident, or individual served)

SAFER Matrix™ Placement	Required Follow-up Activity
HIGH/LIMITED, HIGH/PATTERN, HIGH/WIDESPREAD	• 60-day Evidence of Standards Compliance (ESC) 　- ESC will include Who, What, When, and How sections • ESC will also include two additional areas surrounding Leadership Involvement and Preventive Analysis • Finding will be highlighted for potential review by surveyors on subsequent on-site surveys up to and including the next full triennial survey
MODERATE/PATTERN, MODERATE/WIDESPREAD	• 60-day Evidence of Standards Compliance (ESC) 　- ESC will include Who, What, When, and How sections • ESC will also include two additional areas surrounding Leadership Involvement and Preventive Analysis • Finding will be highlighted for potential review by surveyors on subsequent on-site surveys up to and including the next full triennial survey
MODERATE/LIMITED, LOW/PATTERN, LOW/WIDESPREAD	• 60-day Evidence of Standards Compliance (ESC) 　- ESC will include Who, What, When, and How sections
LOW/LIMITED	• 60-day Evidence of Standards Compliance (ESC) 　- ESC will include Who, What, When, and How sections

Note: If an Immediate Threat to Health and Safety, also known as Immediate Threat to Life (ITL), is discovered during a survey, the organization immediately receives a Preliminary Denial of Accreditation (PDA) and, within 72 hours, must either entirely eliminate the ITL or implement emergency interventions to abate the risk to patients (with a maximum of 23 days to totally eliminate the ITL). Please see "The Accreditation Process" (ACC) chapter within the Comprehensive Accreditation Manual for more information.

Chapter 1 | Understand the Accreditation Process

  II. Implementation
      A. Activities (IC.02.01.01)
      B. Medical Equipment, Devices, and Supplies (IC.02.02.01)
      C. Transmission of Infections (IC.02.03.01)
      D. Influenza Vaccinations (IC.02.04.01)
  III. Evaluation and Improvement (IC.03.01.01)

JCI PCI Standards

Responsibilities (PCI.1, PCI.2)
    I. Resources (PCI.3, PCI.4)
   II. Goals (PCI.5, PCI.6, PCI.6.1)
  III. Medical Equipment, Devices, and Supplies (PCI.7, PCI.7.1)
  IV. Infectious Waste (PCI.7.2, PCI.7.3)
   V. Food Services (PCI.7.4)
  VI. Construction Risks (PCI.7.5)
 VII. Transmission of Infections (PCI.8, PCI.8.1, PCI.8.2, PCI.9)
VIII. Quality Improvement and Program Education (PCI.10, PCI.11)

TOOL OF THE TRADE

- Mock Tracer Form with SAFER™ Matrix

CHAPTER 2

Prioritize Patient Safety

To create a safe work environment, your organization will need a strong safety culture, supported by leadership. Infection prevention and control (IC) involves everyone in your facility. That includes leaders, practitioners, clinical and environmental services staff, facilities directors, risk managers, and others.

Knowing the dangers of infection and how you need to act, react, and interact with everything and everyone in your organization are important to ensure the safety of patients. Whether you're a leader, a nurse, a physician, or a technician, it's vital that you understand who is involved in controlling and preventing infection, and their specific responsibilities. Handling IC issues—and putting patients first—is truly a team effort.

KEY CONCEPTS

- Responsibility for Infection Prevention and Control
- Key Staff and Organizations
- Role of Leadership
- Build a Team for Infection Prevention and Control
- Establish Partnerships
- Safely Integrate Technologies

KEY CONCEPT

Responsibility for Infection Prevention and Control

Joint Commission Infection Prevention and Control (IC) Standard IC.01.01.01 requires your organization to identify individuals responsible for the IC program. Joint Commission International (JCI) addresses this with Prevention and Control of Infections (PCI) Standard PCI.1.

These individuals must oversee the management of infection risks, be proactive in developing strategies for IC, and be able to intervene in situations that pose an immediate threat to staff, patients, visitors, or property. Their duties should be defined by written job descriptions based on your organization's policies and procedures.

Health care organizations must have a strong and consistent IC program that has support from organization leaders. (*See* Chapter 3 for how to create a program).

Leaders' Role in Infection Prevention and Control

The Joint Commission and JCI require leaders and staff to assume responsibility for reducing infection risk. For US organizations, Standard IC.01.01.01, Elements of Performance (EPs) 2–4, offer guidelines for fulfilling that responsibility. International organizations must comply with Standard PCI.4: Organization leadership provides resources to support the IC program. The following is a summary of what your organization leadership is required to do:

- Make sure the organization has identified persons who have authority over the IC program. These individuals should be able to do the following:
    - Guide development of IC policies
    - Guide the implementation of IC policies
    - Oversee the organization's system for identifying, reporting, investigating, and controlling infections and communicable diseases
- Allocate resources for IC, including financial resources, access to information, relevant laboratory resources, and appropriate staff, equipment, and supplies.

smart questions:

Who is responsible for managing IC in your organization? Who is the backup for this person?

Chapter 2 | Prioritize Patient Safety

- Ensure that the organization conducts risk assessments and develops strategies to address those risks (*See* pages 101–103 for a detailed discussion of risk assessments.)
- Assign leaders who have the responsibility for the daily management of IC activities. The number and skill mix of the individuals assigned should be determined by the following:
  - The goals of the IC program
  - The complexity of the organization's IC needs
  - The risks identified in the organization's IC risk assessment
  - The size of the organization

Authority to intervene: Threats from infection can stem from an influx of infectious patients, unsafe conditions, hazardous materials spills, improper hand hygiene, contaminated water, or numerous other sources. So it's critical that someone in your organization has the authority to intervene and is available at all times. Authority to intervene is typically assigned to the same person who manages your facility's IC program.

Backup authority: In a perfect world, your point person should be present at any time to intervene, but we all know it just isn't possible to be on call 24/7. Don't take the risk. Make sure your organization also has another person(s) designated as a backup.

KEY CONCEPT

Key Staff and Organizations

Ultimately, everyone in the organization has some measure of responsibility for IC. The following discusses some key individuals and their roles.

Infection preventionist: Your organization's IC team will rely on the presence and effectiveness of an infection preventionist(s) (or infection control practitioner[s]). This person should have training in how to manage all issues related to IC. An infection preventionist will oversee your organization's policies and procedures regarding infection. This includes how infection is affected by the physical environment, infrastructure, supplies, training personnel, and the community and the geographic location of the organization.

TRY THIS TOOL

Strategies for Engaging Clinicians in IC Activities
Infection preventionists can use this tool to formulate a strategy for engaging physicians and clinicians in IC activities.

Facilities director or engineer: Manages your building or property, including operation, maintenance, and improvements. This person is in charge of compliance with rules and regulations that come with running a health care facility, including those concerning risks for infection. It is critical for the facilities team and the IC team to work together to assess and address risks in the environment that may place patients, staff, or visitors at risk for infection, such as water systems or ventilation.

Clinicians: The primary caregivers in an organization, skilled nursing facility, clinic, or patient's home. They must be educated about and follow good IC practices and policies.

Environmental services (EVS) director: Manages housekeeping, linen distribution, and waste management to minimize infection risks. The environment has been shown to contribute to transmission of pathogens, so it must be cleaned and disinfected continually in patient care, work, and public areas.

Accreditation or safety professional: The person in your organization charged with overseeing overall Joint Commission or JCI compliance.

Key Regulatory Organizations

In the United States, The Joint Commission's IC accreditation standards are complemented by the National Patient Safety Goals (NPSGs). For example, NPSG.07.01.01 requires organizations to comply with US Centers for Disease Control and Prevention (CDC) or World Health Organization (WHO) hand hygiene guidelines. The hand hygiene requirement is part of Goal 7's overall requirement to reduce the risk of health care–associated infections (HAIs). The JCI International Patient Safety Goals (IPSGs)—specifically IPSG.5—address hand hygiene as well.

Along with The Joint Commission and JCI, there are other organizations and agencies with standards, guidelines, or recommendations that affect how you handle IC. Here are some of the key organizations:

Chapter 2 | Prioritize Patient Safety

CDC and NIOSH: The CDC (an operating unit of the US Department of Health and Human Services) conducts research and investigations and works to prevent and control the spread of infectious and contagious disease. It is also involved with the prevention and control of injuries, workplace hazards, disabilities, and environmental health threats. The National Institute for Occupational Safety and Health (NIOSH) is part of the CDC and is responsible for research, education, information, and training in the field of occupational safety and health. The CDC and NIOSH offer guidelines and helpful educational materials related to infection risks.

CMS: For US organizations, accreditation from The Joint Commission can be used to meet certification standards for the US Centers for Medicare & Medicaid Services (CMS). This is known as deemed status or deeming. This is possible because the standards and EPs required for Joint Commission accreditation meet or exceed the standards set by CMS. CMS requirements are most often referred to as Conditions of Participation (CoPs) or Conditions for Coverage (CfCs).

Some Joint Commission standards are required only for organizations seeking to use Joint Commission accreditation for deemed status purposes.

FDA: The US Food and Drug Administration (FDA) ensures the safety of food, cosmetics, drugs for humans (and animals), the blood supply, and medical devices and equipment. The FDA also has enforcement authority, including product recalls, product seizures, and prosecution, so you might receive notices from the FDA on product recalls.

OSHA: The US Occupational Safety and Health Administration (OSHA) is a federal agency that aims to ensure employee safety and health in the United States. Its mission is to prevent work-related injuries, illnesses, and deaths. OSHA works with employers and employees to create better working environments. It has a series of regulations that organizations must follow to ensure employee safety and health, including those related to preventing infections in personnel.

in other words

Deemed status

Health care organizations in the United States that want to participate in and receive payment from the Medicare or Medicaid programs must receive a certification by the US Centers for Medicare & Medicaid Services (CMS) that they are in compliance with the standards set forth in federal regulations. The Joint Commission's standards meet or surpass CMS rules, which are called Conditions of Participation (CoPs). Hence, The Joint Commission is granted "deeming" authority by CMS, which allows it to survey other health care organizations seeking CMS approval and grant them deemed status.

Internationally, health care organizations should adhere to guidelines developed by the WHO or by their country's Ministry of Health; examples include the *Standard Infection Prevention and Control Guidelines* from the United Kingdom's National Health Service, *Guidelines for the Prevention and Control of Infection in Healthcare* from Australia's National Health and Medical Research Council, and the *Technical Guidelines on the Prevention and Control of Hospital Infections* from the Chinese Center for Disease Control and Prevention, among others.

KEY CONCEPT

Role of Leadership

Leaders' ongoing goal should be to continually improve performance at the facility. This includes IC. Leadership positions and titles can vary among health care settings and among different organizations. Examples of some of these include the following:

Executive leadership: This level typically includes the board of directors, as well as the chief executive officer (CEO), chief operating officer (COO), chief medical officer (CMO), and chief nursing officer (CNO), or other administrators.

Responsibilities:
- Setting strategic imperatives
- Serving as role models
- Making IC a priority
- Providing resources for improvement processes
- Heightening awareness of improvement needs for reducing infection risk throughout the organization

Senior leadership: This level includes department chairs, medical and nursing directors, leaders of the organized medical staff, facilities directors, chief financial officer, chief information officer, laboratory directors, nurse managers, director of safety and quality, and accreditation and regulation professionals.

Responsibilities:
- Providing support to the organization's IC program
- Analyzing the current capacity to lead and spread improvement processes to reduce infection risks

Chapter 2 | Prioritize Patient Safety

- Ensuring an infection risk assessment, plan, measurable goals, and reporting system
- Defining how to assign and delegate resources to reach goals
- Monitoring, responding to, and sharing performance improvement reports
- Establishing and maintaining a culture of safety

Frontline leadership: This group may include physicians, clinical nurse specialists and other clinical leaders, infection prevention specialists, staff nurses, patient care managers, pharmacists, and other employees.

Safety Culture

One of the most important functions of leaders is to create and maintain a culture of safety and quality throughout the organization. Promoting an environment that supports teamwork and respect for other people is a vital part of any good organization and is a critical foundation for an effective IC program.

The safety culture of an organization is the product of individual and group beliefs, values, attitudes, perceptions, competencies, and patterns of behavior that determine the organization's commitment to quality and patient safety. Health care organizations that have a robust safety culture are characterized by communications founded on mutual trust, by shared perceptions of the importance of safety, and by confidence in the efficacy of preventive measures. Organizations will have varying levels of safety culture, but all should be working toward a safety culture that has the following qualities:

- Staff and leaders who value transparency, accountability, and mutual respect
- Safety as everyone's first priority
- Behaviors that undermine a culture of safety are not acceptable, and thus should be reported to organizational leadership by staff, patients, and families for the purpose of fostering risk reduction.
- Collective mindfulness is present, wherein staff realize that systems always have the potential to fail, and staff are focused on finding hazardous conditions or close calls at

smart questions:
Who are the frontline leaders in your department?

Organizational Assessment for Safety Culture
Use this tool to assess your organization's commitment to a culture of safety at all levels. If your organization is tolerant of bad behaviors and practices, take a close look at policies and procedures to determine what needs to be addressed or updated.

27

early stages before a patient may be harmed. Staff do not view close calls as evidence that the system prevented an error but rather as evidence that the system needs to be further improved to prevent any defects.
- Staff who do not deny or cover up errors but rather want to report errors to learn from mistakes and improve the system flaws that contribute to or enable patient safety events
- Staff who know that their leaders will focus not on blaming providers involved in errors but on the systems issues that contributed to or enabled the patient safety event

It's important that your leaders evaluate your culture regularly, encourage teamwork, and develop processes and programs that will help create a positive culture. Any behavior that undermines a culture of safety or affects morale can be harmful to staff, patients, and the quality of care, including the IC program. Behavior is something that must be addressed at all levels of the organization, from clinical and administrative staff, to licensed independent practitioners, to management and governing body members.

Leadership commitment to safety must include treating the IC program as a patient safety priority. In addition, staff throughout the organization should feel comfortable reporting concerns or observations related to IC issues or risks and should know how and to whom to report those risks.

Validated Methods to Improve Processes and Systems

The leaders at your organization use data and information to help make the right decisions. Data also help to understand how processes that support safety and quality are performing across your organization. When decisions are backed up by data, your organization is on the right path to achieving the goals that have been set.

For your organization to be successful, it's important to measure and analyze performance data. For example, organizations should track the incidence of HAIs or other IC problems as part of their performance improvement programs. Analyzing the numbers will help leaders find any patterns or trends. This makes it easier to understand the reasons why a process is working well or working poorly. Many types of data are used

Chapter 2 | Prioritize Patient Safety

Establish a Strong Safety Culture

A good starting point for leaders in their efforts to support and bolster the organization's safety culture is an internal survey. Staff responses to a survey on the culture of safety can help leaders begin to understand what the organization's environment is like and can serve as a benchmark for where to start. Survey answers will help identify areas in which the organization is doing well and those that present opportunities for greater focus and improvement.

Analyzing the survey results to find opportunities for quality and safety improvement also enables an organization to develop solutions that align with organizational priorities and needs. The analysis must go deep into local unit levels to ensure that unit-specific solutions are considered. For example, conduct a mock system tracer to evaluate the effectiveness of your organization's sterile processing activities.

After digesting the data, leaders should be involved in developing and implementing unit-based quality and safety improvement initiatives designed to improve the culture of safety. Effective leaders will focus on organizational systems, not employees, to identify latent hazards and weaknesses (such as poor design, lack of supervision, and manufacturing or maintenance defects) and find ways to prevent errors from reaching the patient and causing harm.

When problems or potential hazards are identified, it's vital that leaders do not blame staff for mistakes, lapses, omissions, or other errors. Instead, any issues should be reviewed in the context of the systems related to those issues and identified as opportunities for improvement.

A strong safety culture is built on dignity and respect. Leaders should encourage staff at their organization to be engaged, collaborative, and willing to learn about and improve safety conditions in their units. Unfortunately, many leaders rush to blame employees for adverse events, or are quick to fire people for performance whenever the organization is cited for a safety violation. This will quickly erode the trust between staff and management that is essential to safety culture. Instead, a more thoughtful approach should be taken when dealing with adverse events.

When working to improve hand hygiene compliance, for example, rather than enacting punitive measures, leaders should examine their systems to see how compliance can be improved—for example, the availability and locations of sinks, alcohol-based hand rub dispensers, and gloves; installing visual cues (such as posters) that promote hand hygiene; or providing additional training.

The Joint Commission addresses safety culture in Leadership (LD) Standard LD.03.01.01, which requires leaders to create and maintain a culture of safety and quality throughout the organization. International organizations must comply with Governance, Leadership, and Direction (GLD) Standard GLD.13, requiring leaders to create and support an organizationwide culture of safety program. The Joint Commission's "Patient Safety Systems" (PS) chapter in the *Comprehensive Accreditation Manual* or E-dition also provides a good guideline for leaders.

to evaluate performance, including data on outcomes of care, performance on safety and quality initiatives, patient satisfaction, HAI rates, staff reports of IC or other risks, hand hygiene compliance rates, staff vaccination rates, process variation, and staff perceptions. For IC, data that are valuable to leaders include regular surveillance data with infection rates and

process data displaying compliance with best practices (such as hand hygiene, use of personal protective equipment [PPE], and device-related bundles).

Leadership in data evaluation: The Joint Commission's EPs for Standard LD.03.02.01 define requirements for organizations and leaders to validate methods and improve processes.

Requirements: Leaders set expectations for using data and information for the following:
- Improving the safety and quality of care, treatment, and services
- Decision making that supports the safety and quality of care, treatment, and services
- Identifying and responding to internal and external changes in the environment
- Evaluating how effectively data and information are used throughout the organization

Leadership planning: Planning at your organization should include contributions from all those involved in IC, as well as other interested groups or individuals. Your leaders should be focused on improving patient safety and health care quality and be ready to adapt their plans to changes in the physical environment.

Planning is essential to the following:
- The achievement of short- and long-term IC goals
- Meeting the challenge of external changes, such as infection outbreaks in the community
- The design of services and work processes (for example, cleaning, disinfection, and sterilization of equipment, devices, and supplies)
- The creation of communication channels for reporting IC risks
- The improvement of IC performance
- The introduction of innovation, such as updated IC guidelines or new technologies such as the use of ultraviolet light to reduce *Clostridium difficile* and other HAIs

smart questions:

What IC–related data does your organization collect? How does this help drive improvement in your IC practices and outcomes?

Chapter 2 | Prioritize Patient Safety

Allocate Resources

Your organization leaders will need to allocate resources for the IC program. Joint Commission standards detail three responsibilities of leaders for resource allocation:

Leadership responsibilities for providing resources:

1. Your organization leaders provide access to information needed to support the IC program, such as evidence-based guidelines for hand hygiene and other IC processes, information about local or regional outbreaks, and rates of HAIs in your facility.
2. Your organization leaders provide laboratory resources when needed to support the IC program, such as diagnostic testing to identify infected patients.
3. Your organization leaders provide equipment and supplies to support the IC program, such as PPE, cleaning products, and materials for disinfection and sterilization.

Standardized Ways for Interdisciplinary Teams to Communicate and Collaborate

Communication is vital for all aspects of IC. This means making sure your teams understand your IC safety plan and are up-to-date on any policy and procedure updates. Joint Commission Standard LD.03.09.01 requires organizations to have a program that integrates safety priorities into all processes, functions, and services within an organization, including patient care, support, and contract services. For international organizations, review Governance, Leadership, and Direction (GLD) Standard GLD.4: Organization leadership plans, develops, and implements a quality improvement and patient safety program.

The only way to accomplish this is to communicate and collaborate. Your program should address the responsibility of leaders as we outlined above. It should proactively address potential system failures. It should analyze and work to correct problems that have occurred in your facility. And last, but not least, it should encourage the reporting of adverse events and near misses, both internally and externally.

in other words
Sentinel event

The Joint Commission defines *sentinel event* as a patient safety event (not primarily related to the natural course of the patient's illness or underlying condition) that reaches a patient and results in any of the following:

- Death
- Permanent harm
- Severe temporary harm

JCI defines *sentinel event* as follows: An unanticipated occurrence involving death or serious physical or psychological injury.

For example, if a patient dies after becoming infected with a health care–associated multidrug-resistant organism, The Joint Commission or JCI could designate that incident as a sentinel event.

31

in other words

Patient safety event

A patient safety event is an incident or condition that could have resulted or did result in harm to a patient.

Leadership activities:
- Implement an organizationwide patient safety program that includes IC.
- Create procedures for responding to system or process failures. Responses might include continuing to provide care, treatment, and services to those infected; containing the risk to others; and preserving factual information for subsequent analysis.
- Provide and encourage the use of systems for blame-free internal reporting of a system or process failure, or the results of a proactive risk assessment. For example, a staff member notices that sterile instruments are improperly stored, leading to risk of contamination.
- Make support systems available for staff who have been involved in an adverse event, such as a surgery that led to a fatal surgical site infection.
- Disseminate lessons learned from root cause analyses, system or process failures, and the results of proactive risk assessments to all staff who provide services for the specific situation.
- Encourage external reporting of significant adverse events, including voluntary reporting programs in addition to mandatory programs. Examples of voluntary programs include The Joint Commission Sentinel Event Database, the CDC's National Healthcare Safety Network, and the FDA's MedWatch.

KEY CONCEPT

Build a Team for Infection Prevention and Control

To create an effective IC program, a multidisciplinary, collaborative approach is needed. So how does your organization accomplish this? It starts by forming a team.

Creating a Multidisciplinary Team

One of the most important elements of your program will be a multidisciplinary team. This is a committee or task force responsible for providing guidance to the IC team. A good team will typically include the following:

- Individuals responsible for IC, such as an infection preventionist

Chapter 2 | Prioritize Patient Safety

- Organization leaders
- Physicians
- Nursing leaders and staff from specific clinical specialties
- Patient safety or performance improvement specialists
- Staff responsible for sterile processing
- Staff responsible for equipment maintenance
- Staff responsible for facilities management

Oversight group: The persons designated for oversight roles on the team will be responsible for coordinating the dynamics of program management. This includes implementing intervention strategies, ensuring inclusion of all programs and services, and generating policies and procedures that guide IC compliance. Your organization's infection preventionist will play a key role on the multidisciplinary team and the oversight group.

Oversight team responsibilities:
- Setting criteria to define HAIs
- Establishing surveillance and data collection methods
- Analyzing and reviewing data for possible action
- Implementing risk-reduction strategies
- Reporting process and outcome results
- Coordinating communication with the entire organization to ensure that the program is continuous and proactive
- Maintaining communication with the organizational leader

Initial team actions: Your multidisciplinary team should be trained in IC by your organization, and the roles and responsibilities of each member must be clear. The team should meet regularly to discuss IC topics as well as any reports of infections and infection risks. Policies and procedures and performance improvement action items are other topics that should be on the table.

The first step for the team is to assess the specific infection risk issues in your organization through a proactive and multidisciplinary process. This will help the team establish the focus of the organization's program. After the risk assessment is complete, the team needs to develop a well-defined and specific IC plan that includes measurable goals and objectives to prevent and reduce infection risks (*see* Chapter 3).

33

KEY CONCEPT

Establish Partnerships

Establishing partnerships with experts inside or outside your organization is vital to any IC program. To effectively coordinate activities, the infection preventionist must develop partnerships and obtain the cooperation of managers, point-of-care providers, and other personnel who will accept the responsibility for implementing IC plans. Members may include experts in facility design and ventilation, safety officers, epidemiologists, building engineers, direct care supervisors, risk managers, and building contractors.

Outside partnerships are also something your organization should develop to assist with IC efforts. State hospital associations, state health departments, ministries of health, and CMS Quality Innovation Network and other Quality Improvement Organizations are a good place to start. Try contacting other accredited health care organizations that may have already established best practices that you can adopt and implement into your own program.

Infection preventionists should make a point to stay in contact with state and local public health services. Register for e-mail alerts sent by the health department, the ministry of health, or other government agencies that provide information about illnesses and trends in your community. The health department will also have statistics on population characteristics and health trends that can be helpful when assessing risk. It's also a good idea to establish contacts at state and local health agencies and involve them in your risk assessment process, if possible.

KEY CONCEPT

Safely Integrate Technologies

Many health care organizations are making investments in new technology and processes every day, from adopting electronic health records to new surgical tools. Technology can make your job easier and can certainly assist in your IC efforts. But any time a new innovation is introduced, there is a learning curve and a

Chapter 2 | **Prioritize Patient Safety**

need for a process to ensure that it is introduced properly and used the right way. Failure to integrate technology the right way can jeopardize patient safety. Joint Commission Standard LD.03.03.01 requires your leaders use organizationwide planning to establish structures and processes that focus on safety and quality. Likewise, JCI–accredited organizations must comply with Standard GLD.4, which requires leaders to plan, develop, and implement a quality improvement and patient safety program.

Integrating new technologies and innovation at your facility requires planning. Planning should include contributions from the populations served, from those who work for the organization, and from other interested groups or individuals.

When integrating technology, essential planning requires the following:
- The achievement of short- and long-term goals
- Methods to meet the challenge of external changes
- The design of services and work processes
- The creation of communication channels
- The improvement of performance
- The introduction of innovation

Planning activities must focus on improving patient safety and health care quality and on adapting to changes in the environment. Planning is organizationwide, systematic, and involves designated individuals and information sources. Leaders must evaluate the effectiveness of all planning activities.

With regard to IC technology, there are a number of devices to consider. Health care organizations are demanding more data, and technology has grown to support the need for a more sophisticated approach to data collection and surveillance. Here are a few innovations that are making headway in IC:

Point-of-care testing (POCT): POCT is medical diagnostic testing at or near the point of care and can be performed at the bedside. It involves easy-to-use membrane-based test strips, often enclosed in a plastic test cassette. Already used in blood glucose monitoring and pregnancy testing, POCT can also be

used in the identification of infectious diseases. As POCT technology advances, it should greatly assist infection preventionists working outside of organizations or wherever rapid testing is needed.

Information technology (IT)–based surveillance: There are electronic surveillance systems that can support existing IT platforms. These systems depend on the collection of patient-level information as it is coded, stored, and shared. The use of these systems will help decrease the number of hours that infection preventionists must dedicate to daily surveillance and will assist in data collection, case reviews, and report generation.

Real-time location system (RTLS) technology: RTLS is used to provide immediate or real-time tracking and management of medical equipment, staff, and patients in all types of patient care environments. It can also be used to help optimize the results of IC programs, as well as for staff training. Infection preventionists and other staff at your facility should be specially trained to use RTLS technology.

Hand hygiene monitoring: Hand washing is one of the best ways to prevent the spread of infection. To ensure cleanliness, real-time location systems technologies to monitor hand hygiene are becoming more popular. This technology integrates sensors with dispensers to detect staff use, which can help organizations determine if staff wash their hands before and after patient care.

Data mining: Data-mining programs are an increasingly popular technology used to tackle issues related to HAIs. The programs can help isolate or target infection trends in your facility by linking to a data feed to identify patients with multidrug-resistant organisms or other infections. According to studies, notification of outbreaks and transmission is much faster with data mining.

Choosing Technology
With all the current and impending innovations in technology, how do you decide what to implement? Start with a cost-benefit analysis. Determine how much prospective technology will

Chapter 2 | Prioritize Patient Safety

set your organization back financially, how it will alter work flow if it is integrated, and how effective the technology will be in decreasing infections. Evaluate which infections pose the greatest risk to your environments and what processes effectively mitigate them. Involve staff who would use the technology in the evaluation. After you determine those factors, look for technologies that can help improve your organization's performance in the prevention and control of the identified infections.

TOOLS OF THE TRADE

- Strategies for Engaging Clinicians in IC Activities
- Organizational Assessment for Safety Culture

CHAPTER 3

Make a Plan and Build a Program

The first steps in effective infection prevention and control (IC) and complying with Joint Commission IC standards is to develop an IC plan. The plan must be informed by a risk assessment and evidence-based research. The whole organization should be involved, which means you'll need to generate an effective infrastructure to support the program, create strategies to mitigate infection risk, and develop and maintain continuous surveillance, data collection, and analysis. With a plan in place, your organization can begin to implement policies and processes to control infection.

KEY CONCEPTS

- Start Planning
- Strategies for Assessing Risk
- Establish Goals
- Be Prepared
- Implement Your Plan

KEY CONCEPT

Start Planning

The goal of your IC program is to identify, reduce, and eliminate the risks of acquiring and transmitting infections among patients, staff, and visitors. Creating an effective program means gathering and analyzing information on an ongoing basis, developing collaborative partners, engaging leadership support, and creating a plan. For example, hand hygiene should be integral throughout the organization, and the program should be capable of identifying and quickly investigating clusters of infection, high rates of device-related infections, or exposures to diseases such as tuberculosis. Establishing such a program will improve patient and staff safety, enhance the quality of care, and prevent adverse events.

Effective IC programs have many components that must work together. Suggested components for your plan include the following:

- Gain leadership support for the program.
- Establish an effective infrastructure to support the program.
- Involve the whole organization in IC.
- Establish the focus of the program by assessing risk and creating an IC plan.
- Design strategies to reduce or eliminate infection risk.
- Develop and maintain a continuous surveillance, data collection, and analysis process.
- Evaluate the goals, objectives, and outcomes of the IC program.
- Use evidence-based national guidelines or research by respected organizations.
- Consider laws and mandates that are relevant to the program.
- Write descriptions of IC activities and how processes are evaluated.
- Write processes for investigating outbreaks of infectious diseases.
- Integrate all applicable organization components and functions.
- Develop methods of communication to report IC issues to licensed independent practitioners, staff, visitors, and patients and their families.

Chapter 3 | Make a Plan and Build a Program

- Develop methods for reporting infection surveillance and control information to external organizations.
- Create strategies to prevent the transmission of infectious diseases in your organization.
- Plan for responding to an influx of patients in an emergency.
- Develop methods for reducing the risk of infections associated with medical equipment, devices, and supplies.
- Plan for the immunization of staff and licensed independent practitioners.
- Develop a process for evaluating the effectiveness of the IC plan.

Write the Plan

Joint Commission Infection Prevention and Control (IC) Standard IC.01.05.01 requires all accredited health care organizations to have an IC program that includes a written description of the organization's IC activities, including surveillance, to minimize, reduce, or eliminate the risk of infection. For international organizations, the corresponding standard is Joint Commission International (JCI) Prevention and Control of Infections (PCI) Standard PCI.5: The organization designs and implements a comprehensive infection control program that identifies the procedures and processes associated with the risk of infection and implements strategies to reduce infection risk.

Your organization must develop this written plan using the data gathered from the risk assessments. It must also provide access to information needed to support the plan and identify, prioritize, and document the risks. For more on estimating health risks from exposure to workplace hazards, see the section on risk assessment in Chapter 5.

Written plan elements: Your organization's written IC plan should do the following:
- Identify and address your organization's prioritized risks.
- Identify methods to limit exposure of patients, visitors, and staff to pathogens.
- Identify methods to limit the transmission of infections associated with procedures.

in other
words
Risk assessment

A risk assessment is an examination of a function or process to determine the actual and potential risks and to prioritize areas for improvement.

- Identify methods to limit the transmission of infections associated with the use of medical equipment, devices, and supplies.
- Identify methods for improving compliance with hand hygiene guidelines.
- Identify methods for communicating responsibilities and reporting data to external organizations.
- Detail information regarding current and emerging infections, including evidence-based guidelines.
- Describe the process for investigating outbreaks of infection, including a response to an infectious outbreak or influx of infectious patients.

Your organization should review the written plan annually and when changes occur, such as the addition of a new service.

Evidence-Based Guidelines

Evidence-based guidelines, also called clinical practice guidelines, are based on science and research. They can help leaders, administrators, and practitioners to make decisions for specific clinical circumstances. These guidelines are typically developed by professional health care organizations, government entities, or other groups. They can be used to measure quality, to allocate resources, and to determine cost. They also provide a summary of tested strategies, treatments, and patient safety and other techniques that can aid your organization in IC.

Evidence-based guidelines may help to highlight health problems and deficiencies in clinical services, and leaders at health care organizations may be able to improve the quality of clinical decisions by using evidence-based guidelines. The recommendations can assist clinicians in diagnosing or treating a specific condition such as infection. They can also be used as a reference for quality assurance initiatives, programs, and practice audits.

Use of evidenced-based guidelines is also required by The Joint Commission and JCI. The Joint Commission's IC accreditation standards are complemented by the National Patient Safety Goals (NPSGs), and JCI's PCI accreditation standards are complemented by the International Patient Safety Goals (IPSGs).

in other words

Evidence-based guidelines
These are guidelines that have been scientifically developed based on recent literature review and are consensus driven.

⬇ TRY THIS TOOL

Evidence-Based Guidelines for CLABSI Prevention
The Joint Commission has provided summaries of clinical practice guidelines for central line–associated bloodstream infections (CLABSIs) that can be adapted for your internal use.

Chapter 3 | Make a Plan and Build a Program

Some requirements associated with Goal 7 of the NPSGs require health care organizations to implement evidence-based practices: NPSG.07.03.01 to prevent multidrug-resistant organism (MDRO) infections in organizations; NPSG.07.04.01 to prevent central line–associated bloodstream infections (CLABSIs); NPSG.07.05.01 to prevent surgical site infections (SSIs); and NPSG.07.06.01 to prevent catheter-associated urinary tract infections (CAUTIs).

JCI Standards PCI.3 and PCI.5 require the use of accepted practice guidelines and evidence-based activities, while IPSG.5 requires the adoption and implementation of evidence-based hand hygiene guidelines to reduce the risk of health care–associated infections (HAIs).

Staff involved in these processes must be educated about HAIs and associated guidelines for prevention. (*See* the "Tools of the Trade" in this chapter for examples of evidence-based guidelines.)

KEY CONCEPT

Strategies for Assessing Risk

To mitigate infection risk, your organization must first figure out what those risks are. Risk assessment is a continual and proactive process. Your multidisciplinary team should first review surveillance data to identify risks in each area of your facility. This is done by examining infection rates and results of process surveillance. Examples of process surveillance include tracking staff adherence to isolation precautions, standard precautions, administration of preoperative antibiotics, cleanliness of nutrition services, management of waste, and other issues. Identified risks then must be prioritized according to which of them present the greatest danger.

Your risk assessment must also take into account the regulatory agency requirements by the US Centers for Medicare & Medicaid Services (CMS) and the US Occupational Safety and Health Administration (OSHA), as well as IC guidelines and guidance documents from groups such as the World Health

TRY THIS TOOL

Quantitative Risk Assessment Grid
This tool can be used to identify potential risks in an organization and the probability that they will occur. It can help determine how specific risks should be prioritized and well staff is prepared to mitigate that risk.

43

Organization (WHO), the US Centers for Disease Control and Prevention (CDC), the Association for Professionals in Infection Control and Epidemiology (APIC), the Society for Healthcare Epidemiology of America (SHEA), the Infectious Diseases Society of America (IDSA), ministries of health, and other IC stakeholders.

Assessing risk of infectious disease: Your organization should assess potential outbreaks and possible transmission among patients, licensed independent practitioners, and staff by screening for exposure and/or immunity to infectious disease. When staff or patients have or are suspected of having an infectious disease, the organization should provide further assessment or testing, treatment, and/or counseling. There must also be a written procedure for investigating outbreaks.

Addressing equipment and waste risks: Your organization should determine risk of infections associated with use and reprocessing (cleaning, disinfecting, sterilizing), as well as storing and disposing, of medical equipment, devices, and supplies. It's also vital to minimize the risk of infection by addressing how to properly store and dispose of infectious material.

Addressing communication and information: Methods to communicate responsibilities for preventing and controlling infection to staff, patients, and their families are an important part of assessment. Infection control information should address the safety of everyone in the facility and be available to everyone in the facility, including staff, patients, and their families.

The Risk Assessment Process
When determining risk at your facility, you have many steps to consider. Your risk assessment should do the following:
- Determine the scope of your assessment and select general-risk categories.
- Identify specific risk factors in each category.
- Determine a methodology and risk-scoring system with clear definitions.

Chapter 3 | Make a Plan and Build a Program

- Collect data for the risk analysis.
- Evaluate and score the risk events.
- Determine and identify the risk priorities for the organization.
- Use prioritized risks as the basis for the IC plan.
- Share results with staff and leaders.

Questions about potential infection risk events: Ask questions about the potential for an infection outbreak as you perform your assessment, to make sure your organization is prepared with the answers. Questions that should be asked include the following:

- What are the risks or potential risks that may lead to infections in our organization?
- What is the probability that a risk event will occur?
- If a risk event does occur, how severe should we expect it to be?
- How frequently could the risk event occur?
- What is our organization's ability to identify the risk?
- What kind of response would be required by our organization to reduce or eliminate the risk?
- How well does our leadership support response to risk events?
- How prepared is our organization to respond to challenges right now?
- What effect would a risk event have on our organization, our finances, or the environment?
- How would a risk event affect patients and staff?

Tips for Conducting Surveillance

Surveillance is an important aspect of any good IC program and essential in determining the best intervention strategies for high-risk areas. Surveillance involves collecting data about infections and practices. It should be used to do the following:

- Assess your organization's infection risks for patients, staff, and the environment.
- Identify areas that require further investigation, such as high-risk areas for patients.
- Search for specific diseases.
- Identify infection outbreaks.

in other **words**

Surveillance

Surveillance is a systematic method of collecting, consolidating, and analyzing data concerning the frequency or pattern of, and causes or factors associated with, a given disease, injury, or other health condition. Data analysis is then followed by the dissemination of that information to those who can improve outcomes.

- Determine the effectiveness of processes used to prevent and to control infections and what improvements to systems may be necessary.
- Determine policy and education needs.
- Identify the success of any changes made to a system or process.
- Discover problems, such as new infections or outbreaks.

Being proactive by monitoring will allow your organization to identify, prevent, or mitigate infection risks. For more on surveillance as part of your IC program, see Chapter 5.

What to monitor and collect: Focus your surveillance on infections that place patients or staff at the highest risk. One example of this would be to track only urinary tract infections (UTIs) that involve indwelling catheters in specific high-risk patient populations, instead of tracking all UTIs. Device-related infections are significant risks for patients, and risks related to bloodborne pathogens from exposures to sharps, blood, or body fluids are important for staff.

Types of surveillance: Two common general types of surveillance that your organization should consider are process monitoring and outcome monitoring. These processes will help you to evaluate health care worker performance, clinical practice, and environmental conditions.

> *Process monitoring:* Process monitoring measures how frequently and consistently staff perform IC processes that are approved policies and procedures of the organization. In process surveillance, questions such as the following are answered:
> – How often do physicians or nurses use appropriate barriers when inserting peripheral or central intravenous lines or indwelling urinary catheters?
> – How often is appropriate personal protective equipment (PPE) used?
> – Are preoperative antibiotics administered consistently, prior to surgical incisions?

Chapter 3 | **Make a Plan and Build a Program**

- What is the hand hygiene compliance rate in the organization?
- How clean are patient areas and public areas of the organization?

The purpose of process monitoring is to find out if policies are being followed by staff, which will allow you to identify problems, determine how to educate staff, and then reinforce best practices.

Outcome monitoring: This type of surveillance examines the results of your IC processes and patient care procedures after they are implemented. Outcome measures may include the rates of CAUTIs, SSIs, ventilator-associated events (VAEs), CLABSIs, and catheter-associated bloodstream infections (CABSIs). These rates will allow you to determine the effectiveness of IC practices for patients.

There are many methods of surveillance that can measure processes or outcomes, including the following:

- **Focused incidence surveillance:** This process looks at all new infections in a given time period (for example, during one month or one year) and compares them to previous periods. Among the ways to perform incidence surveillance are the following:
  - Targeted surveillance concentrates on specific patient populations or procedures (for example, targeting infections of patients in ICUs or those at risk for CLABSIs).
  - Problem-oriented surveillance focuses on identified infections and measures their occurrence. When several patients have the same illness, problem-oriented surveillance can determine if an ongoing problem exists and what control measures can be applied to remedy that problem.
- **Prevalence surveillance:** This type of surveillance also monitors infections for a given time period, but it looks at both new and existing infections. The idea is to capture one point or period in time, like a photograph. For example, if you want to look at the number of patients who come to an ambulatory or primary health center with new or continuing

47

malaria in one week, or the number of patients with methicillin-resistant *Staphylococcus aureus* (MRSA) in the surgical ICU during a one-month period, then prevalence surveillance is one way to do that.

The data your organization collects during surveillance efforts will depend on the services you provide and your patient populations, but there are some common areas that you should always consider:

- Infections in patients at the beginning and at the end of the age spectrum (infants to the elderly)
- Sharps or needlestick injuries to staff
- Emerging pathogens
- Hepatitis B or C infections in hemodialysis units
- Infections among immunocompromised patients
- SSIs and other procedure-related infections
- Infections related to implanted devices
- Infections related to indwelling devices (for example, urinary catheters and central intravenous lines)

When collecting data, make sure to involve staff. They will be able to help identify problem areas or offer suggestions on which activities put them and their patients at risk for infections. This will help you to determine what kind of data is accessible and meaningful when you begin your surveillance efforts. Table 3-1 shows a sample hazard assessment using data collected on several elements.

KEY CONCEPT

Establish Goals

Now that your organization has performed a risk assessment, you'll need to use this information to set goals for your IC program.

In addition to complying with established requirements, your organization will want to create its own IC goals, tailored to the unique environment where you and your colleagues work.

The overall goal for your organization's IC program is to identify and reduce risks of infections in patients and workers. To do

Chapter 3 | Make a Plan and Build a Program

Table 3-1. Sample Hospital Infection Control Risk Assessment Hazard Scoring Matrix

Element	Probability 4–Frequent 3–Occasional 2–Uncommon 1–Remote	Risk/Impact Severity Rating		Risk Factor Severity of Effect*	Monitoring, Mitigation, and Remediation Activities P = Policy PI = Process Improvement QC = Quality Control Activity PG = Practice Groups ICC = Infection Control Committee EOC = Environment of Care Committees/ Processes as noted
		Patients 4–Catastrophic Event 3–Major Event 2–Moderate Event 1–Minor Event 0–None/ Nonapplicable	Staff 4–Catastrophic Event 3–Major Event 2–Moderate Event 1–Minor Event 0–None/ Nonapplicable		
Device-related infections in ICU	4	3	1	12	P, PI, QC, PG
Targeted surgical site infections	4	3	1	12	P, PI, QC, ICC, PG
Antibiotic-resistant organisms of epidemiologic significance	4	3	1	12	QC, ICC, PI
Communicable disease reporting	4	1	2	8	P, QC
Blood/body fluid exposure (staff)	4	1	3	12	P, PI, ICC, Employee Health, EOC, Products Selection Committee
Blood/body fluid exposure (patient)	2	3	1	6	Risk Management, ICC
Communicable disease exposure (staff)	4	1	2	8	P, ICC, Employee Health
Communicable disease exposure (patient)	3	2	1	6	ICC, Employee Health, Risk Management
Annual tuberculosis (TB) assessment	4	1	1	4	P, ICC, Employee Health
Influenza vaccination of employees	4	1	2	8	P, PI, ICC, Employee Health
Epidemic (naturally occurring)	1	2	2	4	Emergency Preparedness Plan
Epidemic (bioterrorism)	1	2	2	4	Emergency Preparedness Plan
Standard/isolation precaution	4	2	1	8	P, QC
Construction hazards	3	3	1	9	P
Environmental rounds	3	2	1	6	QC, EOC Committee
Hand hygiene monitoring	3	2	2	12	P, QC, ICC, Patient Safety Committee
Regulated waste management	2	3	1	6	P, PI, QC, ICC, EOC

* To score the risk factor, multiply the probability by the risk/impact rating. The higher the score, the greater the priority.

Adapted with permission of Detroit Medical Center.

that, your first goal must be to improve clinical outcomes using a multidisciplinary team approach, which we discussed in Chapter 2.

Additional recommended goals:
- **Performance improvement.** Establish specific goals to improve performance in certain areas (for example, to increase hand hygiene compliance rates or to increase the number of staff who receive influenza vaccinations by a certain percentage). Other goals could include reduction of SSIs or other types of infections identified in your risk assessment by a certain percentage within a specified time frame (for example, 6 months or 12 months).
- **Executive and leadership support.** A successful IC program requires support and involvement at the highest levels of your organization. A goal to get them on board is crucial.
- **Multidisciplinary team involvement.** As discussed in Chapter 2, your program will need participation from staff across your organization with an understanding of their roles in reducing infections. Involving staff is one of the most important goals of any IC plan.
- **Infection expert training.** Infection preventionists have become more common at health care organizations as the need for formally trained experts in IC has become more apparent.
- **General education in IC.** Health care staff at your organization need to know the basics of IC and understand policies related to IC. It's an important goal to make sure staff are informed of policy updates whenever they are approved, and to let them know when any new technologies can be implemented to minimize infection. Patients should be made aware of the IC practices that staff must follow, such as hand hygiene. Those patients infected with communicable diseases should be educated on how to prevent transmission to others.
- **Outbreak preparedness.** Detecting an outbreak is critical to preventing continual transmission of a potential pathogen to patients, staff, and visitors.

Chapter 3 | Make a Plan and Build a Program

Getting Buy-in from Leadership

The IC programs that receive visible support from leadership are typically the most successful. Although most leaders are not directly involved in the day-to-day operations of the IC program, administrative and clinical leaders must be aware of its functions and goals to properly support it and provide guidance for the development, implementation, and evaluation of the program. The decisions leaders make and the initiatives they support will affect the direction and effectiveness of your program, the quality of care and safety of patients, and the number/amount of resources allocated.

Your leaders' time is valuable. To gain their support, try aligning the IC incentives with those of the organization as a whole. Stress the similarities when discussing the program or proposing new activities. When leaders make decisions, they are largely influenced by effectiveness and efficiency. They will be looking to provide safe, high-quality care while making sure the organization is financially viable. To get them on board, you'll need to let them know what the financial benefits of an IC program are, so expertise in creating a business case for new or ongoing projects is an important skill to have.

Methods for Leaders to Support an IC Program

Following are examples of ways leaders can show their support for their organization's IC program:

- Make IC a visible priority throughout the organization.
- Allocate staff time and resources to the IC program, including the appropriate number of IC professionals who have needed skills—laboratory support, technical support (computers and printers), information technology support, and education and administrative support (data entry and secretarial support).

- Facilitate the infection preventionists' access to patient records, performance-improvement data, and other systems to support surveillance data collection and analysis functions, including the reporting of IC information.
- Support the program by ensuring adequate personal protective equipment (PPE) and supplies for staff to prevent or avoid infections.
- Attend and actively participate in multidisciplinary IC meetings or send a delegate from the leadership team.
- Publicly acknowledge successes in IC, such as reduced infection rates, decreased lengths of stay, or cost savings.
- Serve as a role model to staff (for example, by performing hand hygiene and using appropriate PPE).
- Set expectations for staff (follow IC policies and require attendance at IC–related classes or training sessions).
- Make timely and appropriate education and training efforts a priority for clinical and nonclinical staff.
- Make compliance with IC procedures part of performance evaluations and competency reviews.
- Support coordination of IC efforts within the community and ensure active communication with public health agencies.
- Ensure compliance with regulations and requirements from CMS, state and federal laws, and other authorities as well as recommendations and standards from The Joint Commission.
- Include IC emergencies when developing the organization's emergency management plan.

51

- **Public health reporting.** The members of your IC program team should make it a goal to familiarize themselves with federal, state or regional, and local public health reporting requirements so they can make timely reports.

KEY CONCEPT

Be Prepared

With your team in place, your goals outlined, and your plan ready to be devised and written, you also need to be prepared for the worst. Joint Commission Standard IC.01.06.01 requires your organization to prepare to respond to an influx of potentially infectious patients by doing the following:

- Obtaining current clinical and epidemiological information regarding new infections that could cause an influx of potentially infectious patients
- Having a method in place for communicating critical information to licensed independent practitioners and staff about emerging infections that could cause an influx of potentially infectious patients
- Creating a written description of how your organization will respond to an influx of potentially infectious patients

Organizations outside the United States must comply with JCI Standard PCI.8.1, which requires a process to manage an influx of patients with airborne infections and when negative-pressure rooms are not available.

Prepare for an influx of infectious patients: Many health care organizations have bolstered their response plans for handling major emergencies such as natural disasters (hurricanes, tornadoes), terrorist attacks, or widespread infection outbreaks that may necessitate medical care for a large influx of patients. Having a strategy for a potential influx of infectious patients is required by Joint Commission Emergency Management (EM) and IC standards, as well as JCI Facility Management and Safety (FMS) and PCI standards.

Chapter 3 | Make a Plan and Build a Program

Preparing for a Surge with Current Epidemiology

Emergency situations with infectious patients may arise from injuries sustained during an emergency (such as cholera following a flood), or the infection may be the cause of the emergency itself, such as an infectious disease outbreak like an influenza pandemic. It could also be both. To prepare for a possible surge resulting from infectious disease, your organization must start by obtaining current clinical and epidemiological information regarding risk from new infections and outbreaks. Joint Commission Standard IC.01.06.01 requires your organization to obtain this information from its resources regarding new infections that could cause an influx of potentially infectious patients. To comply with the standard's elements of performance (EPs), you can do the following:

- Communicate about trends regarding significant microbiologic organisms identified in patients, the community, or other health care facilities.
- Access reportable diseases summaries from the state and local health department.
- Share health alert messages from public health officials with facility staff.
- Incorporate the data or information above into a risk assessment.

Your health care organization also needs to be prepared to screen foreign patients for infectious diseases that originated in their countries. When disaster victims from outside the United States are transported here, it can pose an infection risk to your facility. Make sure you have a process for conducting an infectious disease risk assessment of these patients. The risk assessment should be based on the common illnesses in the patient's home country, places they have visited, or environmental circumstances in their country.

Transmissible infections from any part of the world also need to be considered in your emergency response plans. Consider the following:

- Frequency and speed of international travel from each country with emerging infections
- Movement or potential spread of infection (airborne, mosquitoes)

53

- Capabilities of the health care organizations in the country to prevent the spread of an emerging infection (immunization).

Surveillance also plays a crucial role in identifying infection risks, emerging infectious diseases, and outbreaks. You can learn more about surveillance in this chapter (on pages 45–48) and in Chapter 5.

Communication During Emergencies

Many health care organizations like yours are already working hard to meet patient demand on a daily basis. Should a pandemic erupt, managing an increased patient load will be very difficult, particularly for smaller organizations that may have limited access to resources and support. Communication is critical in these situations. The lines of communication need to be strong—before, during, and after an emergency event—and must be transmitted between your organization, the community, emergency responders, and patients to coordinate a sound response to an infectious patient surge.

To keep communication lines open, the infection preventionist (or a designated staff member of your infection control team) will need to monitor information about infectious disease outbreaks, health care alerts, and recent developments in preventing and controlling infectious diseases. This information should be shared with the medical, health and emergency organizations in the area. Local health departments will maintain notification alerts or lists regarding infectious disease outbreaks. This information needs to be communicated to both clinical and nonclinical departments in your organization.

Communication is important when it comes to patient influx too. It starts with staff, who will be needed in an emergency. For those who will be integral to getting an outbreak under control, your emergency communications plan should detail the following:
- Which staff members might be needed during an influx of infectious patients
- How to reach staff to provide clinical and nonclinical services
- Where to reach staff to provide clinical and nonclinical services

Chapter 3 | Make a Plan and Build a Program

- How long staff might be needed
- What arrangements staff should make to be away from home
- What health risks staff will face on duty

The communication plan may also include patients, their loved ones, and the media, particularly if there is an influenza outbreak. Communicating with the media and the general public about where influenza vaccinations are available is crucial to preventing and containing an outbreak. How and when to communicate—and who will do the communicating—and other information related to an emergency is something your IC team or leaders will need to determine. Each situation is different. Many organizations designate an information liaison or communications specialist to speak with these parties.

Tips for Developing a Written Plan for an Influx

If an emergency brings a sudden influx of patients to your health care facility, it's vital that your IC team has established how to provide for the surge and has detailed the response in the plan. Having a written plan is a requirement by The Joint Commission, per Standard IC.01.06.01. Your organization must describe, in writing, how it will respond to an influx of potentially infectious patients. To meet this standard, you'll need to develop materials such as written policies and procedures, program plans, training, checklists, and signage. Evidence of communication regarding these policies, procedures, and plans should be available for review and reference. If your organization decides to accept an influx of patients, the plan should include the procedures that will be used. If your organization decides not to allow an influx of patients in an emergency, the written plan should detail how staff will handle the situation in your community. Whether an influx is accepted or not, the decision should be communicated clearly, both internally and externally.

Accepting an influx: Accepting an influx of potentially infectious patients is a big responsibility. Not only will your written plan need to detail how to bring those patients in safely, it must also describe methods for managing extra patients over an extended period of time. To comply with Joint Commission

and JCI standards, there should be evidence of preparation, supplies, communication, staff training, and education regarding potential influx.

When writing a plan that covers an influx of infectious patients, your IC team should detail the capabilities of your facility. An organization's ability to expand care capabilities in response to sudden or more prolonged demand is known as surge capacity. This includes the ability to accommodate patients for a limited time period during a crisis, as well as longer-term care after the crisis ends. Your written plan should detail surge capacity, which includes the following:

- **Space:** You'll need to know how much available space you have for treatment and services such as triage, vaccinations, and decontamination. Your written plan should detail how much space needs to be dedicated to surge patients and what space requires conversion for an emergency. You should also plan on a backup care site. You'll also have to be prepared for casualties. An additional morgue area may be necessary.
- **Beds:** Include the estimated number of potential patient beds for influx. Remember to include isolation rooms and outpatient areas.
- **Access:** During an emergency your organization should control access. Reduce the number of entry and exit points to the facility and restrict entry to "mission-critical" departments.
- **Staffing:** Detail staffing and specify how many staff members of all types, including volunteers, are needed for an emergency.
- **Isolation rooms:** In an emergency, you'll need to increase the number of isolation rooms available for patients and determine how to separate the isolation and decontamination areas from the rest of your facility. Include plans for mechanical and ventilation systems to support isolation. Air intakes and exhaust must be separated from the main facility.
- **Supplies and equipment:** A supply of personal PPE, such as face masks, gloves, and gowns, needs to be ready at a moment's notice. Your plan should detail procedures for obtaining additional PPE quickly during an emergency. This means contacting suppliers to make sure they have a means

Chapter 3 | **Make a Plan and Build a Program**

of delivering your equipment in a hurry. Make sure to test and maintain emergency power supplies and other backup systems.

- **Traffic and patient flow:** You must anticipate an increased volume of patients, emergency vehicles, and parking. Your plan needs to detail alternate traffic flow patterns to accommodate the increased activity.
- **Clear passageways:** The plan should detail a procedure for ensuring that exits are unobstructed and have appropriate signage. Corridors need to be free of clutter in an emergency.
- **Utilities:** Your written plan should include contingency building utility systems in case the main systems fail. Consider alternatives for running electricity, water, ventilation, fuel sources, medical gas/vacuum systems, sanitation, and so on.
- **Legality:** It's important to know the legal capacity to deliver health care services in emergency situations requiring influx. This should be mentioned in the plan.

The written plan should also cover methods for preventing the infection from entering your organization during a surge. Should an infectious disease outbreak occur, your plan should offer guidance on the following:

- Preventing the infection from being introduced into your facility
- Recognizing if the infection has been introduced
- Containing the spread of the infection if it is introduced

Prepare for Patients Requiring Isolation

To prevent infection from spreading to staff, to other patients, to visitors, or to areas in your organization, isolation is critical. Isolation standards require that patients, visitors, and staff be protected from infections via barriers or isolation rooms. An alternative isolation method is a high-efficiency particulate air (HEPA) filtration system that functions at the rate of at least 12 air exchanges per hour. Using HEPA filters is considered a temporary solution to inadequate numbers of isolation rooms. No matter which type of isolation room your organization uses, it requires procedures for managing patients who may spread infection through the air.

smart questions:

Does your health care facility accept an influx of patients in an emergency? If so, is there a written plan?

57

Anterooms, or transitional rooms, are often used as waiting areas to isolation rooms. They help to prevent the spread of infection during an outbreak. Anterooms must be properly designed, placed, and pressurized, depending on the patients receiving care. If there is an infectious disease outbreak, the room and anteroom should be negative pressure. If the patient is immunocompromised (for example, a radiation victim), the isolation room and anteroom would be in an area where air is forced out of the room (positive pressure).

Organizations should also have protocols in place to determine how supplies are provided and managed for isolated patients, such as clothing, bedding, linens, food, water, and eating utensils. Emergency supplies of these items should be stored or easy to obtain. Make sure to keep an inventory of supplies.

According to WHO's 2014 guidelines, Infection Prevention and Control of Epidemic- and Pandemic-Prone Acute Respiratory Infections in Health Care, additional preparation inside an isolation room or area requires that your organization do the following:

- Ensure that appropriate hand-washing facilities and hand hygiene supplies are available.
- Stock the sink area with suitable supplies for hand washing, and with alcohol-based hand rub, near the point of care and the room door.
- Ensure adequate room ventilation.
- Post signs on the door indicating that the space is an isolation area.
- Ensure that visitors consult the health care worker in charge (who is also responsible for keeping a visitor record) before being allowed into the isolation areas. Keep a roster of all staff working in the isolation areas, for possible outbreak investigation and contact tracing.
- Remove all nonessential furniture and ensure that the remaining furniture is easy to clean and does not conceal or retain dirt or moisture within or around it.
- Stock the PPE supply and linen outside the isolation room or area (for example, in the change room). Setup a trolley outside the door to hold PPE. A checklist may be useful to ensure that all equipment is available.

Chapter 3 | Make a Plan and Build a Program

Preparing for an Influx of Infectious Patients Requiring Airborne Infection Isolation

Recognize that an influx of patients requiring an airborne infection illness (negative airflow) environment might exceed current physical plant capabilities. In an effort to begin a planning process, the following information may provide the beginnings of an evaluation process you could include in your plan. The information noted below is not comprehensive but should serve as a beginning for dialogue with the facility emergency manager, facilities engineering personnel, safety officer, and executive staff:

- Identify existing airborne infection isolation (negative airflow) environments and determine capacity.
- Ensure status of negative airflow using smoke stick or other similar method.
- Evaluate the existing seal of each room. Check seals around windows and electrical outlets.
- Select an appropriate area for surge capacity (wing or separate building), taking the following into consideration:
  - The existing heating, ventilating, and air-conditioning (HVAC) system
  - Location of adjacent populations in all directions, particularly high-risk areas such as oncology and nurseries
  - Controlled access for traffic patterns
  - Accessibility from areas of first patient encounter (for example, emergency department, admissions)

- The existing utility and service capabilities:
  - Electrical outlets on emergency backup power
  - Oxygen delivery
  - Medical gas
  - Suction
  - Sinks
  - Commodes
- Develop a floor plan that indicates blocks of rooms/areas served by each air handler.
- Develop a plan that indicates blocks of rooms/areas served by each ventilation exhaust fan.
- Develop a schematic for each air-handling unit (AHU) system indicating flow to each room, return airflow, associated exhaust system, and any recirculation pattern. This information may make you reconsider your initial selection of an appropriate area.
- Identify where air is exhausted and ensure that it is at least 25 feet away from any air intake and 100 yards from other entrances into the facility.
- Evaluate existing equipment, including ventilators, portable suction, and additional oxygen tanks.
- Evaluate existing supplies, including personal protective equipment and suction supplies.

- Place appropriate waste bags in a bin. If possible, use a touch-free bin. Ensure that used or dirty bins remain inside the isolation rooms. Ensure that waste is discarded per organization policy.
- Place a puncture-proof container for sharps disposal inside the isolation room or area.
- Keep the patient's personal belongings to a minimum. Keep water pitchers and cups, tissue wipes, and all items necessary for attending to personal hygiene within the patient's reach.

- Dedicate noncritical patient-care equipment (for example, stethoscope, thermometer, blood pressure cuff, sphygmomanometer) to the patient, if possible. Thoroughly clean and disinfect patient-care equipment that is required for use by other patients before use.
- Place an appropriate container with a lid outside the door for equipment that requires disinfection or sterilization.
- Keep adequate equipment required for cleaning or disinfection inside the isolation room or area and ensure scrupulous daily cleaning of the isolation room or area.
- Set up a telephone or other method of communication in the isolation room or area to enable patients, family members, or visitors to communicate with health care workers. This may reduce the number of times the workers need to don PPE to enter the room or area.

Educate Staff on Influx Procedures

When an emergency arises, and an influx of patients comes through the front door, health care personnel at your facility need to be well prepared to prevent transmission of infection to others or themselves. The middle of an epidemic is not a good time to make sure everyone knows what to do. To ensure that staff are competent and prepared, education that focuses on recognition, response, containment, and communication is key. It's important to standardize education among health care workers to ensure that staff across health care facilities in your community are taught the same disciplines. You want everyone to be on the same page should an outbreak occur. Standardized education for influx may include instruction on the following:

- The role of microorganisms in disease and how they are transmitted in health care settings
- The types of emerging infections, bioterrorism agents, and pandemic influenza to look out for
- The standard and transmission-based precautions for patient contact in your facility
- Protocols for health care workers to protect themselves from infection
- Methods for health care workers to prevent transmission of infection to patients

Chapter 3 | **Make a Plan and Build a Program**

- Problem-solving skills for recognizing, containing, and preventing infection transmission
- Patient placement, cohorting, transport, and discharge protocols
- Proper PPE use
- Hand hygiene
- Triage procedures
- Patient decontamination procedures
- Quarantine and isolation procedures
- Procedures for laboratory testing of infected patient specimens
- Surge capacity protocols and procedures
- Postmortem procedures
- Sanitation procedures
- Plans and backup plans for supplying utilities, food, and water to an influx of patients and staff
- IC plans for alternative care sites

The infection preventionist and the IC team will be responsible for getting health care workers up to speed on the procedures required to ensure the safety of patients and the community during an emergency. Education efforts might start with the assessment of staff needs and involve training programs, frequent communication, and evaluation. Staff must understand their roles in IC efforts, particularly in an emergency situation with an influx of patients.

KEY CONCEPT

Implement Your Plan

An IC plan must be implemented to mitigate or eliminate the risk of infection. After your IC team has performed its risk assessments and developed a written plan (see pages 41–42 in this chapter), the next step is to put that plan into action. By implementing the right processes, your organization will be able to reduce infection risks for its patients and their loved ones, staff, and visitors. Putting your IC plan into effect requires a collaborative team effort among departments and staff to practically apply it.

Implementing strategies to reduce infection risks is certainly a challenge. Those organizations that have achieved success typically rely on the following approaches:

1. Creation of team activities, driven by staff
2. Administration and leader buy-in and commitment
3. Consistent use of evidence-based practices
4. Assurance that supplies are available for IC needs
5. Education and competency of staff regarding IC issues and procedures
6. Use of monitoring and measurement of practices and outcomes via surveillance
7. Effective communication, including feedback of surveillance findings to staff
8. Ongoing evaluation of interventions and continuous improvement activity
9. Celebrations of success

Allocate Resources

To make the IC plan work, you'll need adequate resources. These include access to information, relevant laboratory resources, and appropriate PPE and supplies. It's a good idea to catalog the resources you have and the resources you will need based on your risk assessment of the organization (*see* page 59). How does your organization decide which resources will go to IC and not to other programs? Resource allocation can be difficult. Your organization leadership will make the final determination on what will be allocated. That decision will largely depend on the evidence-based recommendations and implementation strategies for the plan that you present to the administration (*see* the "Leadership Buy-In" sidebar on page 51).

Standard IC.01.02.01 requires leaders to allocate needed resources for the IC program. The EPs for IC.01.02.01 include the following:

- The health care organization provides access to information needed to support the IC program.
- The health care organization provides laboratory resources when needed to support the IC program.
- The health care organization provides equipment and supplies to support the IC program.

Chapter 3 | Make a Plan and Build a Program

Similarly, JCI provides Standard PCI.4, which requires organization leaders to allocate resources to support the IC program, including staffing, information management systems, and other resources; and Standard PCI.8.2 requires organization leaders to develop an influx plan.

Benchmarking and Data Collection

As part of your IC program you'll need to collaborate with different departments to not only collect surveillance data but also to analyze it. A good way to analyze those data is by benchmarking, which compares your organization's data with best-practice data from a reliable, science-based source. You can choose internal or external benchmarking for your IC data.

Internal benchmarking: The first method is to benchmark against reliable internal data that have yielded positive results. Internal data are valuable because they will demonstrate performance improvement at your organization over time. To establish performance rates, you'll need to first generate baseline information to which you can compare future data. By comparing data to the initial baseline over time, you will be able to tell if an infection rate is decreasing or increasing.

External benchmarking: The method compares your organization's data with external data sources. External benchmarking will reveal if your organization's rates of infection are higher or lower than that of other health care facilities with comparable populations or settings.

Whether you are benchmarking with internal or external data, it's important to use standardized methods for identifying infection and collecting data. This "apples to apples" comparison will give you an accurate picture of how your IC program is performing.

Reporting data: The data and information you collect to improve your processes can also be used to help identify risks of infections, outbreaks, new diseases, and other threats. Make sure you are in contact with public health or national agencies, which often require and rely on health care organizations like yours to report trends and patterns. This information is vital to

mitigating infections, not just in your facility or community but also worldwide. Part of your IC plan should include procedures for complying with local reporting laws.

Identify Areas for Continued Improvement

To ensure an effective IC program, your team will need to continually evaluate your plan's objectives to make sure they are being met and to improve them if needed. As stated in the section above, benchmarking is a good way to learn how your plan is performing by the numbers and will help you identify weak spots in your plan. Performing risk assessments on a regular basis or whenever new risks are introduced is also important to minimize those risks and to identify other potential risks to your community.

Joint Commission Standard IC.01.03.01, EP 2, requires your organization to review and identify risks at least annually and whenever significant changes occur with input from, at a minimum, IC personnel, medical staff, nursing, and leadership. In the JCI standards, risk assessment is addressed at Standard PCI.5. The idea is to ensure that policies and procedures are developed by a multidisciplinary team, the members of which will offer different perspectives on the risk evaluation process. Those performing a risk assessment should consider the following:

- New technologies
- Established and new procedures and policies
- Medications such as vaccines and chemotherapy
- High-risk invasive procedures
- Populations served and services provided
- Environmental issues
- Training and education for staff
- Community characteristics
- Each care setting, (for example inpatient, outpatient, office-based care)
- Available IC resources

Schedule evaluations: Evaluations should be planned and conducted regularly throughout the year to ensure that the plan

Chapter 3 | Make a Plan and Build a Program

is achieving the desired goals. For best quality-of-care performance results, the organization should establish and maintain a schedule for reviewing the goals, activities, and outcomes. Such evaluations should conclude with a statement of the current effectiveness of the plan and any actionable recommendations to address opportunities for improvement.

Communicate evaluation findings: Findings from the evaluation should be communicated at least annually to the individuals or interdisciplinary group that manages the program. The organization should use these findings when revising the IC plan.

> ### Why Conduct Risk Assessments?
> - To improve patient safety
> - To improve staff safety
> - To improve efficiency
> - To identify staff training issues
> - To develop hypotheses for anticipating potential risks
> - To justify a need for implementing new IC activities or continuing current activities
> - To avoid potentially adverse events

Prevention Initiatives

More than any other goal, preventing infections from even happening is the most important. CMS (for US organizations), The Joint Commission (IC.02.01.01, EP 2), and JCI (PCI.8) require your organization to use standard precautions, including the use of PPE to reduce the risk of infection. Ministries of health in some countries may have similar requirements. Standard precautions are universally practiced, and general infection prevention and control measures are designed to protect patients, staff, and others against potential exposure to infectious agents. Standard precautions include safe injection practices, proper medication handling, and use of PPE. *See* Chapter 4 for more on standard precautions and use of PPE.

Safe injection practices: Unsafe injection practices affect thousands of patients each year, particularly in outpatient settings. Your prevention initiatives need to focus on reducing

TRY THIS TOOL

Injection Safety Checklist
This checklist is appropriate for inpatient and outpatient settings and can be used to assess adherence to safe injection practices.

this risk. The CDC offers guidelines related to safe injection practices that apply to the use of needles, cannulas that replace needles, and intravenous delivery systems. To administer injections safely, do the following:

- Use the aseptic technique to avoid contamination of sterile injection equipment. Follow proper infection control practices during the preparation and administration of medications. Aseptic technique means using practices and procedures to prevent contamination from pathogens. It involves applying the strictest rules to minimize the risk of infection.
- Do not administer medications from the same syringe to multiple patients, even if the needle or cannula on the syringe is changed.
    - Needles, cannulas, and syringes are sterile, single-use items that should not be reused for another patient, or to access a medication or solution that might be used for a subsequent patient.
    - Use fluid infusion and administration sets (for example, intravenous bags, tubing, connectors) for one patient only and dispose of appropriately after use.
- After a device has been used to enter or connect to a patient's intravenous infusion bag or administration set, consider the syringe or needle/cannula to be contaminated.
- Use of single-dose/single-use vials is strongly encouraged for patient safety. Assign medication packaged as a multidose vial to a single patient.

Medication management: Properly handling all opened and unopened medication vials is an important part of preventing infection. Medication vials should be used in one area, so the chain of custody and sterility is maintained. They should not be transported to another area. The CDC states that the medication area should be clean and not adjacent to areas where potentially contaminated items are stored, such as used syringes or needles. Any item that could have come in contact with blood or body fluids or water should not be in your medication preparation area. For small medication preparation areas, barriers between water supply and preparation areas, such as a splash guard, are recommended to prevent contamination.

Chapter 3 | Make a Plan and Build a Program

Personal protective equipment (PPE): PPE is essential to preventing exposure to potentially infectious material, reducing the risk of transmission of bloodborne pathogens, and averting cross-contamination during patient care. To reduce the risk of infections, your organization must identify the minimal required PPE for protection based on risks associated with infection and specific diagnoses and environmental conditions. You'll also need to monitor PPE use to ensure that staff are using it regularly and properly. Staff members should also be able to show competent use of PPE. *See* Chapter 4 for more details on the proper use of PPE.

Prevention Initiative Materials

The Health Research & Educational Trust (HRET) and the Agency for Healthcare Research and Quality (AHRQ) have had significant impact on prevention initiatives. A variety of tools and education materials can be found here:
http://www.hret-hiin.org/topics/index.shtml
http://www.ahrq.gov/professionals/index.html

Develop a Communication Plan for IC Issues

Part of your IC program must include communication about the goals and objectives of the plan, performance improvement initiatives, and any surveillance data you've gathered. Communicating IC initiatives that reduce risk and improve safety will help your organization achieve compliance throughout the organization. You should have ongoing communication regarding IC issues with all physicians, nurses, clinical and support staff, volunteers, related health care organizations, regulatory and accreditation bodies, and patients and their families. Communication will not only help improve safety by reducing the risk of infections and outbreaks, it will facilitate collaboration with staff, leadership, and your community. Developing and writing a proactive communication plan will be helpful in ensuring that communication reaches all of your audiences in a timely manner. *See* Table 3-2 for some communication methods.

67

Table 3-2. Communication Methods and Advantages of Each Type

Communication Types	Methods	Situations	Advantages
Direct verbal communication	1-to-1 verbal exchange Telephone information Meetings Unit rounds	When an important infection-related issue needs an immediate response Unit huddles or debriefs—identified outbreak, increased incidence, or rare organism PowerPoint or other presentation at IC, medical, or nursing staff meetings Rounding on units—device use rounds	Ability to ask questions Opportunity to actively engage stakeholders Education in the moment Connects activities back to the patient Gives immediate feedback Promotes discussion
Policies, procedures, guidelines	Policy or guideline development IC bundles Checklists	When a practice change or new evidence-based guideline is implemented When important information must be clearly detailed	Describes accountability Standardizes practice
Electronic communication	E-mail information—electronically Electronic reminders or alerts Internal websites with rates posted	Routine infection reports When a repository of information is required for multiple persons to access	Efficient Can provide feedback to ascertain when messages are read
Written newsletters or publications	Administrative dashboard information disseminated quickly	When information needs to be displayed	Can also be sent electronically
Educational presentations or offerings	Formal method to disseminate information in a structured manner	When new knowledge or information requires a structured approach	Structured approach

IC, infection prevention and control.

Additional committees that govern your organization—leadership, patient safety, nursing committees, governing board, environment, and so forth—should also receive the most current IC information.

The Joint Commission requires communication of responsibilities for preventing and controlling infection to licensed independent practitioners, staff, visitors, patients, and families in Standard IC.02.01.01, EP 7. International organizations should review JCI Standard PCI.11.

- **Communicate IC issues to staff and licensed independent practitioners:** Orientation is a good way to provide IC information to staff in the organization. Infection

Chapter 3 | **Make a Plan and Build a Program**

preventionists can offer face-to-face interaction, handouts, visual aids, and videos to help staff better understand IC issues and their roles in prevention and control. It can also be used to inform staff about strategic goals and IC policies and procedures at your facility.

Your infection preventionist should work with physicians, licensed independent practitioners, and other medical staff to integrate IC into their processes. Information can be shared during committee and medical group meetings. You may also consider creating a monthly newsletter to be sent via e-mail or through your organization's intranet to reach those physicians and other licensed independent practitioners who are not on site often.

Consider the following information that should be communicated to stakeholders:

- **Communicate surveillance, prevention, and control information to staff:** Joint Commission Standard IC.02.01.01, EP 8, requires your organization to report infection surveillance, prevention, and control information to the appropriate staff. JCI has a similar requirement at PCI.11, Measurable Element (ME) 1. Reporting will help foster a culture of patient safety and minimize or eliminate infections. Your IC Committee members are responsible for sharing data and information with the staff. They can communicate that information in a number of ways, including the following:
  - Informing direct health care providers about the number and identity of patients and residents who acquired particular infections on their units each month
  - Providing direct health care providers with aggregate data and trends over time for infections or compliance rates with care processes
  - Providing information to modify physician, nursing, and other health care staff behavior for improved compliance with an organization's IC protocols
  - Empowering patients and residents to speak up when health care providers fail to wash their hands or clean an injection port prior to accessing an intravenous (IV) port

69

– Communicate with personnel at other facilities: Communication with other health care workers at other facilities can make a difference in patient care. Patients are often moved from one part of your health care organization to another, from one organization to another, or from an organization to an outpatient or ambulatory care setting, so it's vital to let health care workers involved in their care know about any related IC information.

Joint Commission Standard IC.02.01.01, EP 10, requires your organization to inform any receiving organization about a patient who has an infection requiring monitoring, treatment, and/or isolation. The information communicated should be directed to the internal staff at the receiving organization, who can distribute it to direct care providers.

- **Communicate to families and visitors:** It is essential that families of patients be included in the IC communication program to help them best care for their family members and protect themselves and others from infection. A patient's family is very important to his or her care. Families and outside caregivers participate in many daily activities, such as hygiene or providing meals to the patient. To help prevent infection from spreading, communicate important safety protocols and other information on infection to families and visitors through brochures, pamphlets, and videos. One-on-one verbal communication with family members and visitors is also helpful. When language barriers exist or with pediatric patients, pictures are particularly helpful in addition to the other communication methods mentioned above.
- **Reporting to the state health department or ministry of health:** Reporting information to the local health department and/or the state licensing and certification division, regarding persons with communicable diseases such as tuberculosis is required by law or regulation in all states and by Joint Commission Standard IC.02.01.01, EP 9. However, what you must report is very different from state to state. More than 30 states require reporting HAIs through the CDC's National Healthcare Safety Network (NHSN). You can find a list of those states here: http://www.cdc.gov/hai/stateplans/required-to-report-hai-NHSN.html

Chapter 3 | **Make a Plan and Build a Program**

CMS also requires all acute care facilities to report HAIs through NHSN. A list of current reporting requirements can be found here: http://www.cdc.gov/nhsn/PDFs/CMS/CMS -Reporting-Requirements.pdf

Ministries of health in several countries have similar reporting requirements for specific diseases within certain time frames. Your organization should be well aware of these requirements.

To comply with your local, state, and national agency require- ments, you'll need to continually update your IC practices. Having a system to regularly check for updated requirements is critical. Make sure to subscribe to alerts, e-mails, newsletters, and communication networks used by regulatory agencies. Maintain communication with agencies or ministries of health to ensure getting the most current information.

Implement Evidence-Based Practices

If you are an IC practitioner or infection preventionist, your ultimate responsibility is to minimize the risk that patients or staff will contract an infection in the organization. One of the best ways to do that is to create practices based on scientific evidence. Fortunately, you have a variety of resources to help you consider evidence-based practices, including the guidelines from the Healthcare Infection Control Practices Advisory Committee (HICPAC) of the CDC and other science-based IC recommendations by that agency and guidelines or mandates from the ministry of health in your country.

HICPAC guidelines and those from some countries' ministries may include performance measures that will help you develop performance measures for your IC plan. HICPAC documents can be found on the CDC/HICPAC Guidelines Library webpage at https://www.cdc.gov/infectioncontrol/guidelines/index.html. They include prevention guidance for the following (titles and headings are as shown on the Guidelines Library webpage):

- **Basic Infection Prevention and Control**
    - Disinfection and sterilization
    - Environmental infection control
    - Hand hygiene
    - Isolation precautions

- **Antibiotic Resistance**
  - Multidrug-resistant organisms (MDRO)
- **Device-associated**
  - Catheter-associated urinary tract infection (CAUTI)
  - Intravascular catheter-related infection
- **Procedure-associated**
  - Organ transplantation
  - Surgical site infection (SSI)
- **Disease/Organism-specific**
  - Ebola
  - Influenza – A virus (novel)
  - Influenza (seasonal)
  - MERS-CoV
  - Norovirus
  - Pneumonia prevention
  - Smallpox pre-event vaccination
  - Tuberculosis (TB)
- **Healthcare Worker Guidelines**
  - HBV infected healthcare workers
  - HBV protection and postexposure management
  - HIV occupational exposure management
  - Infection control in healthcare workers
  - Vaccines for healthcare workers

Many professional organizations base their organizational policies on evidence-based prevention strategies. APIC offers a series of implementation guides at www.apic.org/Professional-Practice/Implementation-guides. The guides cover such topics as CAUTI and CLABSI.

Chapter 3 | Make a Plan and Build a Program

TOOLS OF THE TRADE

- Evidence-Based Guidelines for CLABSI Prevention
- Quantitative Risk Assessment Grid
- Injection Safety Checklist

Additional Resources

CDC 2007 Guideline for Isolation Precautions: Preventing Transmission of Infectious Agents in Healthcare Settings (Updated October 2017)
IC practitioners and infection preventionists and their colleagues need every possible tool at their disposal to prevent and mitigate infections. These updated guidelines by the CDC provide advice for infection control staff, epidemiologists, administrators, nurses, and other health care providers: https://www.cdc.gov/infectioncontrol/pdf/guidelines/isolation -guidelines-H.pdf.

Preventing Unsafe Injection Practices
Safe injection practices are a set of recommendations within standard precautions, which are the foundation for preventing transmission of infections during patient care in all health care settings, including hospitals, long term care facilities, ambulatory care, home care, and hospice. The most recent CDC guideline outlining safe injection practices is in the 2007 Guideline for Isolation Precautions: Preventing Transmission of Infectious Agents in Healthcare Settings (see the link above). The safe injection practices guideline can also be read on-screen at the CDC's Isolation Precautions webpage: https://www.cdc.gov /infectioncontrol/guidelines/isolation/index.html.

PART II: Comply with Infection Prevention and Control Standards and Goals

CHAPTER 4

Prevent Transmission of Infections

THE BIG IDEA

Anyone who enters a health care organization may be exposed to infectious pathogens, and then can expose patients, other staff members, and visitors. A hallmark of a good infection prevention and control (IC) program is making sure specific processes are in place to protect everyone who walks into your health care facility against the transmission of infectious disease. That means trying to stop pathogens before they have a chance to spread.

KEY CONCEPTS

- Use Caution: Prevent Exposure
- Infectious Disease in Health Care Staff
- Influenza Vaccinations
- Hand Hygiene Guidelines

> **TRY THIS TOOL**
> **Components for Compliance with Joint Commission IC Standards**
> Use this tool to quickly assess compliance with Standards IC.02.03.01 and IC.02.04.01 in your organization.

smart questions:
Is your health care organization proactively screening staff for exposure to infectious diseases?

in other words
Standard precautions
Standard precautions are prevention and control measures to protect against potential exposure to infectious diseases.

KEY CONCEPT

Use Caution: Prevent Exposure

To prevent exposure, your organization will need to make proactive health screenings or immunity to infectious disease through vaccinations available to licensed independent practitioners and staff who may come in contact with infections at the workplace. This is required by Joint Commission Infection Prevention and Control (IC) Standard IC.02.03.01 and IC.02.04.01. In addition, Joint Commission International (JCI) Prevention and Control of Infections (PCI) Standard PCI.5 requires a comprehensive IC program that identifies the processes and procedures associated with the risk of infection and implements strategies to reduce those risks in patients and staff.

Precautionary measures to protect staff and patients from exposure to emerging infectious diseases include the following:
- Education, training, and retraining and ensuring competencies on the most current guidance from the US Centers for Disease Control and Prevention (CDC), the World Health Organization (WHO), or your country's ministry of health for specific infectious diseases
- Provision of readily accessible and appropriate personal protective equipment (PPE)
- Contact with local and state departments of health for information. This is imperative to protect the health and well-being of the patient, resident, family, and health care worker.

Standard Precautions
To prevent the spread of infection at your organization you need to start with standard precautions. Standard precautions are prevention and control measures to protect against potential exposure to infectious diseases. These measures include PPE, sharps safety, and respiratory and cough etiquette. (*See* the "Prevention Initiatives" section in Chapter 3.)

Standard precautions should be practiced universally at your health care organization, whether it be a hospital, outpatient and ambulatory setting, behavioral health care facility, nursing care center, home care setting, hospice, or laboratory. For more

Chapter 4 | Prevent Transmission of Infections

about standard precautions visit the WHO website at www
.who.int/infection-prevention/tools/en/ or the CDC's website at
www.cdc.gov/hai to find a variety of IC tools and guidance.

Safe Use of Sharps

Occupational exposure to bloodborne pathogens from needlesticks and other sharps injuries is a serious problem. When staff
become exposed to infectious pathogens, they run the risk of
transmitting those infections to patients. Sharps injuries have
transmitted more than 20 pathogens, including hepatitis B virus
(HBV), hepatitis C virus (HCV), and human immunodeficiency
virus (HIV). To prevent transmission of infectious disease, the
CDC says health care workers in your organization need to be
prepared and be aware of the potential risks. Here are some
precautionary steps that your IC team should take:

Prepare: Before staff even handle sharps, it's important to
make sure your environment is set up to prevent injuries by
doing the following:
- Organizing work areas with appropriate sharps disposal
  containers within reach
- Making sure staff work in well-lit areas
- Offering training to staff on how to use sharps safety devices
- Assessing any hazards before handling sharps and get help
  if needed

Be aware: It's also important to remind staff to be aware of
what they are doing when they handle sharps. Teach them to
do the following:
- Keep exposed sharps in view
- Be mindful of people around them
- Stop if they feel rushed or distracted
- Focus on the task at hand
- Avoid hand-passing sharps
- Use verbal alerts when moving sharps
- Watch for sharps in linens, in beds, on the floor, or in
  waste containers
- Report sharps injuries or sharps hazards to help prevent
  future injuries

smart questions:

*In what ways do
occupational exposures
to pathogens
endanger patients?*

> **TRY THIS TOOL**
>
> **Sharps Program Assessment Worksheet**
> Use this worksheet to perform a baseline assessment of processes in your organization that support a sharps-injury prevention program. This worksheet can serve as a tool for discussing improvements that may lead to a reduction in sharps-related injuries in health care staff.

Containing sharps: Safe handling of sharps when in use isn't the only precaution you and your colleagues will need to consider. Properly disposing of used needlesticks and sharps is equally important. Disposing of sharps with care requires disposing of devices in rigid sharps containers.

Containers to dispose sharps should be disposable, closable, as well as leak and puncture resistant. In addition, containers should be:

- **Accessible and convenient:** Containers should be readily available to workers who use, maintain, or dispose of sharp devices. They should be conveniently placed within the workplace, and convenient for the user and the facility.
- **Plainly visible:** Staff should be able to see how full the container is, the proper warning labels, and color coding.
- **Labeled properly:** In the United States, the containers should have hazard warning labels in accordance with the US Occupational Safety and Health Administration's (OSHA's) Bloodborne Pathogens Standard. When appropriate, labels should display the biohazard symbol and the word "Biohazard." View a quick reference guide to the standard at https://www.osha.gov/SLTC/bloodbornepathogens/bloodborne_quickref.html.
- **Easy to store and assemble:** Containers should be simple to use, assemble, and store. Consider staff training to make sure everyone knows how to perform these tasks.

> ### Sharps Injuries
>
> Sharps injuries in US hospitals are often due to the use of the following:
> - Hypodermic needles/syringes
> - Suture needles
> - Winged-steel (butterfly-type) needles
> - Blood collection needles
> - Scalpels
> - IV stylets
> - Other devices, including glass

Chapter 4 | **Prevent Transmission of Infections**

Personal Protective Equipment

PPE is essential to preventing exposure to potentially infectious material, reducing the risk of transmission of bloodborne pathogens, and averting cross-contamination during patient care. To reduce the risk of infections, your organization must identify the minimal required PPE for protection based on risks associated with infection. You'll also need to monitor PPE use to ensure that staff are using it regularly and properly. Staff members should also be able to show competent use of PPE.

In some cases, patients and visitors should also be educated on the use of PPE. Patients with respiratory illnesses may be asked to wear a mask, for example. Visitors to immunocompromised patients or some surgical patients may be asked to don masks, gloves, and/or gowns.

PPE for infection control includes the following:

- **Masks and respirators:** Masks protect staff, patients, or visitors from infectious material getting into their noses and mouths. Respirators filter air before it is inhaled.
- **Face and eye protection:** Goggles will protect individuals from infectious material splattering in their eyes. Face shields will protect your eyes, nose, and mouth.
- **Gloves:** Vinyl, latex, or nitrile gloves will protect individuals when touching patients, handling infectious materials, or touching contaminated surfaces.
- **Gowns:** Protects individuals from getting potentially infectious material on their clothing.
- **Shoe covers:** Protects individuals from getting potentially infectious material on their shoes or stepping in hazardous material.
- **Head covers:** Provides an additional barrier to a potentially infections environment.

in other words

Personal protective equipment

Personal protective equipment (PPE) is worn to minimize exposure and transmission of infectious pathogens.

smart questions:

Does your organization have a process for educating patients and visitors about the use of PPE?

Sequence for Donning Personal Protective Equipment

HOW TO SAFELY REMOVE PERSONAL PROTECTIVE EQUIPMENT (PPE) EXAMPLE 1

There are a variety of ways to safely remove PPE without contaminating your clothing, skin, or mucous membranes with potentially infectious materials. Here is one example. **Remove all PPE before exiting the patient room** except a respirator, if worn. Remove the respirator **after** leaving the patient room and closing the door. Remove PPE in the following sequence:

1. GLOVES
- Outside of gloves are contaminated!
- If your hands get contaminated during glove removal, immediately wash your hands or use an alcohol-based hand sanitizer
- Using a gloved hand, grasp the palm area of the other gloved hand and peel off first glove
- Hold removed glove in gloved hand
- Slide fingers of ungloved hand under remaining glove at wrist and peel off second glove over first glove
- Discard gloves in a waste container

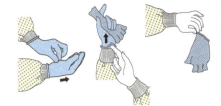

2. GOGGLES OR FACE SHIELD
- Outside of goggles or face shield are contaminated!
- If your hands get contaminated during goggle or face shield removal, immediately wash your hands or use an alcohol-based hand sanitizer
- Remove goggles or face shield from the back by lifting head band or ear pieces
- If the item is reusable, place in designated receptacle for reprocessing. Otherwise, discard in a waste container

3. GOWN
- Gown front and sleeves are contaminated!
- If your hands get contaminated during gown removal, immediately wash your hands or use an alcohol-based hand sanitizer
- Unfasten gown ties, taking care that sleeves don't contact your body when reaching for ties
- Pull gown away from neck and shoulders, touching inside of gown only
- Turn gown inside out
- Fold or roll into a bundle and discard in a waste container

4. MASK OR RESPIRATOR
- Front of mask/respirator is contaminated — DO NOT TOUCH!
- If your hands get contaminated during mask/respirator removal, immediately wash your hands or use an alcohol-based hand sanitizer
- Grasp bottom ties or elastics of the mask/respirator, then the ones at the top, and remove without touching the front
- Discard in a waste container

5. WASH HANDS OR USE AN ALCOHOL-BASED HAND SANITIZER IMMEDIATELY AFTER REMOVING ALL PPE

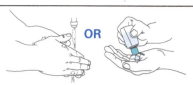 OR

PERFORM HAND HYGIENE BETWEEN STEPS IF HANDS BECOME CONTAMINATED AND IMMEDIATELY AFTER REMOVING ALL PPE

CS250672-E

Chapter 4 | **Prevent Transmission of Infections**

Respiratory Hygiene

Respiratory illnesses can be transmitted by people who cough or who have congestion or rhinorrhea (runny nose). To limit these transmissions, it's important to contain the respiratory secretions of those who shows signs of infection. This can be achieved through respiratory hygiene and cough etiquette.

Hygiene etiquette actions:

- Cover noses and mouths when coughing or sneezing.
- Use tissues and discard them in the nearest trash receptacle after use.
- Wash hands with antiseptic soap or an alcohol-based hand rub after contact with contaminated objects or respiratory secretions.

The supplies mentioned above—tissues and antiseptic soap—must be made readily available in your facility. The CDC recommends that health care organizations do the following:

- Provide tissues and no-touch receptacles for used tissue disposal.
- Provide conveniently located dispensers of alcohol-based hand rub. Ensure that supplies for hand washing (for example, soap, disposable towels) are consistently available at sinks.

The locations of supplies and how they can be replenished should be a part of your IC plan.

In addition, it's important to promote respiratory hygiene and cough etiquette by adding informative signs to your facility that illustrate the actions. Signage will serve as a reminder for staff, patients, and visitors to comply with these IC protocols. Place the signs in waiting areas and entrances for maximum visibility. (*See* the example on page 82.)

Transmission-Based Precautions

Earlier in this chapter we discussed standard precautions, which give you a solid, but basic base for preventing transmission of infections. They are a Joint Commission/JCI–required response to pathogens suspected or identified within your organization's service setting. Transmission-based precautions include contact precautions, droplet precautions, and airborne precautions.

81

CDC 'Cover Your Cough' Poster

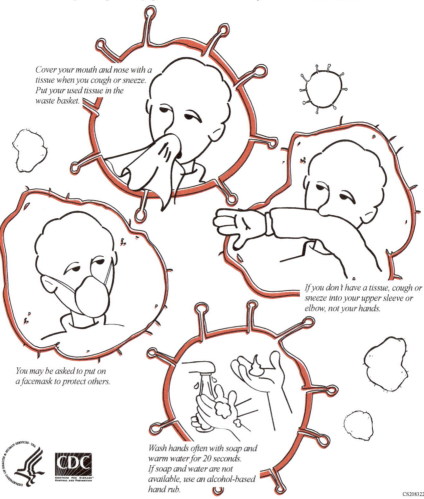

This CDC poster is an example of signage that organizations can use to remind staff, patients, and visitors about respiratory hygiene and cough etiquette.

Chapter 4 | **Prevent Transmission of Infections**

Contact precautions:

- Ensure appropriate patient placement in a single-patient space or room if available. In acute care hospitals, if single rooms are not available, use the recommendations for alternative patient placement in the Guideline for Isolation Precautions: Preventing Transmission of Infectious Agents in Healthcare Settings from the CDC (*see the* Additional Resources section). In long-term and other residential settings, if private rooms are not available, make room placement decisions that balance risks to other patients. In ambulatory settings, place patients requiring contact precautions in an exam room or cubicle as soon as possible.
- Wear a gown and gloves for all interactions that may involve contact with the patient or the patient's environment. Don PPE upon room entry and properly discard before exiting to contain pathogens.
- Limit movement of patients outside of the room to medically necessary purposes. When transport is necessary, cover or contain the infected areas of the patient's body. Dispose of contaminated PPE and perform hand hygiene prior to transporting patients. Don clean PPE to handle the patient at the transport location.
- Use disposable equipment for each patient. If equipment must be used for multiple patients, make sure to clean and disinfect it before use on each.
- Prioritize cleaning and disinfection of patient rooms (daily or prior to use by another patient in an outpatient setting). Focus cleaning on frequently touched surfaces and equipment.

Droplet precautions:

- Droplet precautions are necessary when an individual has a condition that causes infectious agents to be spread through contact with or inhalation of small droplets, such as coughing or sneezing.
- Ensure appropriate patient placement in a single room if possible. In nursing care centers and other residential settings, make decisions regarding patient placement on a case-by-case basis, considering infection risks to other patients in the room and available alternatives. In ambulatory settings, place patients who require droplet precautions in an exam room or cubicle as soon as possible and instruct

patients to follow respiratory hygiene/cough etiquette recommendations.
- Use PPE appropriately. Don mask upon entry into the patient room or patient space.
- Limit transport and movement of patients outside of the room to medically necessary purposes. If transport or movement outside of the room is necessary, instruct the patient to wear a mask and follow respiratory hygiene/cough etiquette.

Airborne precautions:
- Airborne precautions should be used when an individual is suspected or confirmed as having an infection that could be transmitted through pathogens in the air, such as measles or tuberculosis.
- Ensure appropriate patient placement in an airborne infection isolation room (AIIR) constructed according to the Guideline for Isolation Precautions. In settings where airborne precautions cannot be implemented, mask patients and place them in private rooms with the door closed to reduce the likelihood of airborne transmission.
- Restrict susceptible health care personnel from entering rooms of patients known or suspected to have measles, chickenpox, disseminated zoster, or smallpox. This can include staff who have been exposed to one of these pathogens, staff who have not been vaccinated, or staff who otherwise may lack immunity to these illnesses.
- Use PPE—a fit-tested National Institute for Occupational Safety and Health (NIOSH)–approved N95 or higher-level respirator for health care personnel when in contact with patients requiring airborne precautions.
- Limit movement of patients outside of the room to medically necessary purposes. If transport outside an AIIR is necessary, instruct patients to wear surgical masks and observe respiratory hygiene/cough etiquette.
- Immunize patients and staff as soon as possible following unprotected contact with vaccine-preventable infections.

Chapter 4 | Prevent Transmission of Infections

KEY CONCEPT

Infectious Disease in Health Care Staff

If a licensed independent practitioner or staff member is suspected of having occupational exposure to an infectious disease that puts others at risk, your organization must provide them with an assessment and potential testing, treatment, work restrictions, or counseling.

Make sure that any health care workers at risk of contracting an infectious disease at your facility receive the support needed to assess the severity of an exposure and to determine how to address it. To do this quickly, your IC team should be aware of the types of exposures that may affect staff and create specific plans to address them right away so that they can be managed immediately and effectively. For example, staff members may be exposed to patients suffering from tuberculosis, bloodborne pathogens such as HBV, or even more rare diseases, such as Ebola.

Exposed health care workers referred to counselors, such as the individual responsible for occupational safety and health or an infection preventionist, should clearly understand your organization's policies regarding work restrictions and when they can return to their duties. The counselor should help provide this information, as well as any required documentation and reports, and assist in communicating the status of exposed workers to leadership.

- **Identifying suspected staff infection during an infectious disease outbreak:** Should an outbreak occur; your organization should consider hosting daily conference calls or meetings to make sure all departments are on the same page and are collaborating to ensure patient and staff safety. During an outbreak, your organization should have a method of identifying any workers who may be exposed, or show symptoms of infection, so they can be isolated and treated. This will help prevent further spread of the disease.

85

KEY CONCEPT

Influenza Vaccinations

Why vaccinate staff: Annual vaccination for influenza is a safety measure to prevent the transmission of influenza from health care workers to patients, other staff, and visitors to your facility. According to the CDC, vaccinations may also reduce the following:
- The number of personnel continuing to work while they are ill (also known as presenteeism)
- Staff illness and absenteeism
- Influenza-related illness and hospitalization, particularly among people at increased risk for severe influenza illness

Another reason to vaccinate staff is to protect children. Influenza is very dangerous for young people, particularly infants. Since 2010, the CDC estimates that flu-related hospitalizations among children younger than 5 years ranged from 7,000 to 26,000 in the United States. Children younger than 6 months old cannot receive an influenza vaccination. The best way to protect them is to make sure people around them are vaccinated, which means it's important to immunize staff—as well as family members and visitors—who come into contact with babies. Visit the CDC website at https://www.cdc.gov/flu/protect/children.htm to view resources for vaccinating children.

Having staff vaccinated can also benefit the safety of older patients, who are particularly susceptible to infectious diseases. Influenza is a serious threat for older patients in long term care. The CDC estimates that between 71% and 85% of seasonal flu-related deaths have occurred in people 65 years and older. Visit the CDC website at https://www.cdc.gov/flu/toolkit/long-term-care/importance.htm to view resources for vaccinating older adults.

Strategies for promoting and encouraging vaccination:
Vaccinating health care workers for influenza is a challenge. Most organizations have a lot of busy staff with varied schedules, so getting everyone to comply requires a lot of effort and takes time. If you're an infection preventionist, you have a key role in working with leadership to come up with a proactive

Chapter 4 | Prevent Transmission of Infections

immunization program. So where do you start? Below are a few of the strategies offered by the Minnesota Department of Health.

Ensure convenient access
- Have mobile carts make several trips to each unit during all shifts.
- Offer peer vaccination on patient care units.
- Hold flu shot clinics at several different dates and times.
- Coordinate shot clinics with other activities like benefit fairs and meetings to make it easy for workers to attend.
- Promote night shift and evening shift vaccination.

Engage staff
- Keep a positive attitude! This is key for engaging staff and promoting vaccine.
- Communicate in person and give employees opportunities to ask questions one-on-one. This helps get doubtful employees vaccinated.
- Promote vaccination to all employees whether they provide direct patient care or not.
- Break down vaccination rates by department and post them in the facility for all to see.
- Encourage department managers to take ownership for their rates and create friendly competition.
- Offer employees a small token as an incentive, such as a piece of candy. Keeping patients healthy is the best incentive.
- Be sure education modules are fun and catchy. Use themes with matching slogans. For example, the World Health Organization's slogan, "Immunize for a Healthy Future: Know. Check. Protect." (Know reasons to vaccinate and types of necessary vaccinations. Check whether you have received necessary vaccinations or need boosters. And protect yourself and others by getting vaccinated.)
- Enlist experienced nurses to act as "flu champions" who tirelessly vaccinate, "beat the drum," advertise, encourage, and "bug people" to promote the vaccine.

Make flu vaccination a workplace expectation
- Inform new employees of the flu vaccination expectation at the time of hire and make vaccine available to them right away if possible.

TRY THIS TOOL

Strategies for Increasing Influenza Vaccination Rates Among Health Care Workers
A Joint Commission Resources flu vaccine challenge blog revealed some helpful strategies for increasing vaccination rates among health care staff that are outlined in this tool.

87

- Seek strong administrative support in order to achieve high rates. Ask administrators to send out an e-mail or write a reminder in the employee newsletter.
- Incorporate flu vaccine education into the annual training curriculum for employees.

Focus flu vaccination on the community
- Offer vaccination to immediate family members of employees. This helps shift the focus off the self-interest of the health care worker and toward the importance of protecting the community.
- Participate in conducting a back-to-school flu vaccination campaign to help promote early vaccination in addition to employee programs.

Consider using declination forms
- Use declination forms only after exploring all other options.
- Expect to get less pushback than you might think for mandating declination forms.
- Offer declination forms online so employees can access them at their convenience.
- Offer a preservative-free vaccine to those who declined, to help persuade them to get vaccinated.
- Try framing the declination form as a tool to record reasons employees choose not to get vaccinated rather than as a way to refuse.
- Have Human Resources follow up with employees who don't return declination forms. Explain to employees that if they do not fill out a declination for an extended period of time, they can be removed from the work schedule.
- Use the declination form as an educational tool to explain the rationale for flu vaccination and to rebut specific reasons for declining.
- Require declination forms to be returned so you can collect data on specific reasons for declining and target education toward them.
- Suggest, as one facility did, that the medical director express strong support for the initiative by seeing employees for free if they need a medical exemption and by offering them one-to-one counseling.

TRY THIS TOOL

Declination of Influenza (Flu) Vaccination
A declination form, such as this one, should be easily accessible to employees who decline immunization.

Chapter 4 | Prevent Transmission of Infections

- Be aware that implementing mandatory declination requires diligence in addition to support from all departments and employee unions.

The CDC recommends that health care personnel get their flu vaccine early in the fall, by the end of October. It takes about two weeks after vaccination for antibodies to develop, so having staff vaccinated early in the influenza season will better protect them before the flu strikes the community.

In addition, WHO recommends that health care staff working in international settings and who may be at risk of infection from bloodborne viruses, be immunized for HBV early in their career.

You can find other recommended influenza prevention measures at the CDC's Influenza Vaccination Coverage page at https://www.cdc.gov/flu/fluvaxview. For WHO's strategies for protecting health care workers from bloodborne viruses, *see* http://apps.who.int/iris/bitstream/handle/10665/68354 /WHO_BCT_03.11.pdf?sequence=1&isAllowed=y&ua=1.

KEY CONCEPT

Hand Hygiene Guidelines

CDC and WHO guidelines: The guidelines from both the CDC and WHO offer comprehensive guidance and recommendations on infection control related to hand hygiene.
- **The CDC's Guideline for Hand Hygiene in Health-Care Settings:** The CDC's guideline provides health care workers with a review of scientific data regarding hand washing and hand antisepsis in health care settings, including the following:
  - Indications for hand washing and hand antisepsis
  - Hand hygiene technique
  - Surgical hand antisepsis
  - Selection of hand hygiene agents
  - Skin care
  - Other aspects of hand hygiene

89

It also provides specific recommendations to promote improved hand hygiene practices and reduce transmission of pathogenic microorganisms to patients and personnel in health-care settings. You can download the guideline and educational slide sets at https://www.cdc.gov/handhygiene/providers/guideline.html.

The WHO Guidelines on Hand Hygiene in Health Care: The WHO guidelines offer a thorough review of evidence on hand hygiene in health care. They also give specific recommendations to improve hygiene practices and reduce transmission of pathogenic microorganisms to patients and health care workers. The guidelines are aimed at administrators, public health officials, and health care workers, and they are designed to be used in any setting in which health care is delivered either to a patient or to a specific group. You can download the WHO guidelines and supplementary material at http://www.who.int/infection-prevention/publications/hand-hygiene-2009/en/.

Organizations that have successfully improved hand hygiene compliance have used multidisciplinary approaches based on the CDC and WHO guidelines. Some of those strategies include the following:

- Ensuring management and leadership support of hand hygiene programs
- Educating health care personnel, patients, residents, and visitors about the importance of hand hygiene and how to properly clean hands
- Providing appropriate hand hygiene facilities and products in convenient locations
- Hanging posters and other reminders to clean hands by sinks, in restrooms, and other strategic locations
- Encouraging patients, residents, and families to speak up and ask health care personnel to clean their hands
- Creating and implementing incentive programs and competitions
- Measuring compliance with hand hygiene procedures and providing feedback to health care personnel on their performance
- Engaging champions of hand hygiene to lead campaigns

Chapter 4 | **Prevent Transmission of Infections**

- Using staff role models
- Instituting a culture of patient safety and leadership and health care personnel accountability

The recommendations are designed to improve hand hygiene practices of health care workers and to reduce transmission of pathogenic microorganisms to patients and personnel in health care settings. Each recommendation is categorized on the basis of existing scientific data. For example, here is the CDC ranking system for categorizing hand hygiene recommendations:

Category IA – Strongly recommended for implementation and strongly supported by well-designed experimental, clinical, or epidemiologic studies.

Category IB – Strongly recommended for implementation and supported by certain experimental, clinical, or epidemiologic studies and a strong theoretical rationale.

Category IC – Required for implementation, as mandated by federal or state regulation or standard.

Category II – Suggested for implementation and supported by suggestive clinical or epidemiologic studies or a theoretical rationale.

No Recommendation – Unresolved issue. Practices for which insufficient evidence or no consensus regarding efficacy exist.

You can see how these recommendations are made at https://www.ncbi.nlm.nih.gov/books/NBK144035/. Each rating is assigned to recommendations of hand hygiene under various categories, including the following:
- Indications for hand hygiene
- Hand hygiene technique
- Recommendations for surgical hand preparation
- Selection and handling of hand hygiene agents
- Skin care
- Use of gloves
- Other aspects of hand hygiene

Center for Transforming Healthcare Hand Hygiene Project and TST Solutions

The Joint Commission Center for Transforming Healthcare began work on its first Targeted Solutions Tool improvement project: addressing failures in hand hygiene. The Hand Hygiene Project focuses on improving and sustaining hand hygiene compliance. Hand hygiene is critically important to safe, high-quality patient care. Unfortunately, many infections are transmitted by health care personnel. To sustain improvement and make a difference, a simple slogan or campaign is not enough; demanding that health care workers try harder is not the answer. Comprehensive, systematic, and sustainable change is the only solution.

Targeted Solutions Tool® (TST®) for Hand Hygiene

The Targeted Solutions Tool (TST) is an innovative application developed by the Center that guides health care organizations through a step-by-step process to accurately measure their organization's actual performance, identify their barriers to excellent performance, and direct them to proven solutions that are customized to address their particular barriers.

Clinicians found the TST to be effective and easy to implement within their organizations. Each hospital faced distinctive challenges in hand hygiene practices, which were addressed through the comprehensive, data-driven TST process.

To learn more about the Hand Hygiene Project and TST, visit https://www.centerfortransforming healthcare.org/tst_hh.aspx.

Chapter 4 | **Prevent Transmission of Infections**

- Educational and motivational programs for health care workers
- Governmental and institutional responsibilities

TOOLS OF THE TRADE

- Components for Compliance with Joint Commission IC Standards
- Sharps Program Assessment Worksheet
- Strategies for Increasing Influenza Vaccination Rates Among Health Care Workers
- Declination of Influenza (Flu) Vaccination Form

Additional Resources

Standard Precautions Guide
The CDC offers a quick reference guide to using standard precautions: https://www.cdc.gov/infectioncontrol/basics/standard-precautions.html.

CDC Workbook for Sharps Prevention
The CDC offers a *Workbook for Designing, Implementing, and Evaluating a Sharps Injury Prevention Program* to help health care facilities prevent needlesticks and other sharps-related injuries to health care personnel: https://www.cdc.gov/sharpssafety/pdf/sharpsworkbook_2008.pdf.

For more detailed guidance on transmission-based precautions, download the CDC's *Guideline for Isolation Precautions* at https://www.cdc.gov/infectioncontrol/pdf/guidelines/isolation-guidelines-H.pdf.

The CDC provides *Guidance for the Selection and Use of Personal Protective Equipment (PPE) in Healthcare Settings* here: https://www.cdc.gov/HAI/pdfs/ppe/PPEslides6-29-04.pdf.

It also offers a *Guide to Infection Prevention for Outpatient Settings* that includes appropriate use of PPE at https://www.cdc.gov/infectioncontrol/pdf/outpatient/guide.pdf. PPE guidance from the World Health Organization is available at http://www.who.int/csr/resources/publications/ebola/ppe-guideline/en/.

The CDC site also has videos, slides, and posters that demonstrate how to safely put on, use, and remove PPE.

CHAPTER 5

Prevent Health Care–Associated Infections

Health care–associated infections (HAIs) are among the most common adverse events in health care and have long been recognized as being problematic for patient safety. Although HAIs are a well-known cause of sickness and death, patients continue to be infected at a high rate.

in other words

Health care–associated infections

Health care–associated infections (HAIs) are infections patients can acquire while receiving medical treatment in a health care facility.

KEY CONCEPTS

- Using National Patient Safety Goal 7 as a Guide for Preventing HAIs
- Risk Assessment
- Staff Education
- Patient and Family Education
- Surveillance
- Implement Evidence-Based Practices

KEY CONCEPT

Using National Patient Safety Goal 7 as a Guide for Preventing HAIs

The Joint Commission and Joint Commission International (JCI) require organizations to implement strategies to prevent infections and monitor their efforts to ensure ongoing compliance. It is crucial for your organization to measure the effectiveness of its infection prevention and control (IC) program as a part of its ongoing performance improvement activities. In addition to The Joint Commission's IC standards and JCI's Prevention and Control of Infections (PCI) standards, organizations will be evaluated on their intent to meet National Patient Safety Goal (NPSG) 7 (US organizations) or International Patient Safety Goal (IPSG) IPSG.5.

International Patient Safety Goal 5

Joint Commission International's International Patient Safety Goals also address HAIs in Goal 5: Reduce the risk of health care–associated infections. The requirement under this goal, IPSG.5, focuses on adherence to evidence-based hand hygiene guidelines and is discussed in Chapter 4. Hand hygiene is essential to preventing many types of infections, including some of those addressed under The Joint Commission's National Patient Safety Goal 7. These include catheter-associated urinary tract infections (CAUTIs), bloodstream infections, and others.

In addition to hand hygiene (discussed in Chapter 4), National Patient Safety Goal 7 offers guidance on key IC areas:

Multidrug-resistant organisms (MDROs): MDROs are bacteria that become resistant to antibiotics. They develop when antibiotics are taken longer than necessary or when they are not needed. The more the antibiotics are used, the more likely it is that resistant bacteria will develop and infect patients. MDROs spread from patient to patient via hands of health care workers, or by objects that have been touched such as door handles, bed rails, bedside tables, and medication carts. The presence of MDROs is on the rise in health care organizations. MDROs are covered in NPSG.07.03.01.

▼ TRY THIS TOOL

Compliance Assessment Checklist for NPSG 7
Organizations can use this form to assess compliance with National Patient Safety Goal 7.

▼ TRY THIS TOOL

Risk Assessment Matrix for Prevention of MDROs
Use this tool to assess your organization's risk for MDROs

in other words

Multidrug-resistant organisms

Multidrug-resistant organisms (MDROs) are bacteria that resist treatment with more than one antibiotic. They can cause serious infections, particularly in older patients or patients who are very ill.

Chapter 5 | **Prevent Health Care–Associated Infections**

National Patient Safety Goal 7

The Joint Commission 's National Patient Safety Goal 7 includes guidance regarding the most common and dangerous HAIs in health care facilities:

- **NPSG.07.04.01**: Implement evidence-based practices to prevent central line–associated bloodstream infections.
  - Elements of Performance for NPSG.07.04.01
    1. Educate staff and licensed independent practitioners who are involved in managing central lines about central line–associated bloodstream infections and the importance of prevention. Education occurs upon hire or granting of initial privileges and periodically thereafter as determined by the organization.
    2. Prior to insertion of a central venous catheter, educate patients and, as needed, their families about central line–associated bloodstream infection prevention.
    3. Implement policies and practices aimed at reducing the risk of central line–associated bloodstream infections. These policies and practices meet regulatory requirements and are aligned with evidence-based standards (for example, the Centers for Disease Control and Prevention (CDC) and/or professional organization guidelines).
    4. Conduct periodic risk assessments for central line–associated bloodstream infections, monitor compliance with evidence-based practices, and evaluate the effectiveness of prevention efforts. The risk assessments are conducted in time frames defined by the health care organization, and this infection surveillance activity is organizationwide, not targeted.
    5. Provide central line–associated bloodstream infection rate data and prevention outcome measures to key stakeholders, including leaders, licensed independent practitioners, nursing staff, and other clinicians.
    6. Use a catheter checklist and a standardized protocol for central venous catheter insertion.
    7. Use a standardized supply cart or kit that contains all necessary components for the insertion of central venous catheters.
    8. Perform hand hygiene prior to catheter insertion or manipulation.
    9. Use maximum sterile barrier precautions during central venous catheter insertion.
    10. For adult patients, do not insert catheters into the femoral vein unless other sites are unavailable
    11. Use an alcoholic chlorhexidine antiseptic for skin preparation during central venous catheter insertion unless contraindicated.
    12. Use a standardized protocol to disinfect catheter hubs and injection ports before accessing the ports.
    13. Evaluate all central venous catheters routinely and remove nonessential catheters.

- **NPSG.07.05.01**: Implement evidence-based practices for preventing surgical site infections.
  - Elements of Performance for NPSG.07.05.01
    1. Educate staff and licensed independent practitioners involved in surgical procedures about surgical site infections and the importance of prevention. Education occurs upon hire, annually thereafter, and when involvement in surgical procedures is added to an individual's job responsibilities.
    2. Educate patients, and their families as needed, who are undergoing a surgical procedure about surgical site infection prevention.

National Patient Safety Goal 7 *continued*

3. Implement policies and practices aimed at reducing the risk of surgical site infections. These policies and practices meet regulatory requirements and are aligned with evidence-based guidelines (for example, the Centers for Disease Control and Prevention (CDC) and/or professional organization guidelines).
4. As part of the effort to reduce surgical site infections:
   - Conduct periodic risk assessments for surgical site infections in a time frame determined by the hospital.
   - Select surgical site infection measures using best practices or evidence-based guidelines.
   - Monitor compliance with best practices or evidence- based guidelines.
   - Evaluate the effectiveness of prevention efforts.
5. Measure surgical site infection rates for the first 30 or 90 days following surgical procedures based on National Healthcare Safety Network (NHSN) procedural codes. The organization's measurement strategies follow evidence-based guidelines.
6. Provide process and outcome (for example, surgical site infection rate) measure results to key stakeholders.
7. Administer antimicrobial agents for prophylaxis for a particular procedure or disease, according to methods cited in scientific literature or endorsed by professional organizations.
8. When hair removal is necessary, use a method that is cited in scientific literature or endorsed by professional organizations.

- NPSG.07.06.01: Implement evidence-based practices to prevent indwelling catheter-associated urinary tract infections (CAUTI).
  - **Elements of Performance for NPSG.07.06.01**

1. Educate staff and licensed independent practitioners involved in the use of indwelling urinary catheters about CAUTI and the importance of infection prevention. Education occurs upon hire or granting of initial privileges and when involvement in indwelling catheter care is added to an individual's job responsibilities. Ongoing education and competence assessment occur at intervals established by the organization.
2. Educate patients who will have an indwelling catheter, and their families as needed, on CAUTI prevention and the symptoms of a urinary tract infection.
3. Develop written criteria, using established evidence-based guidelines, for placement of an indwelling urinary catheter. Written criteria are revised as scientific evidence changes.
4. Follow written procedures based on established evidence-based guidelines for inserting and maintaining an indwelling urinary catheter. The procedures address the following:
   - Limiting use and duration
   - Performing hand hygiene prior to catheter insertion or maintenance care
   - Using aseptic techniques for site preparation, equipment, and supplies
   - Securing catheters for unobstructed urine flow and drainage
   - Maintaining the sterility of the urine collection system
   - Replacing the urine collection system when required
   - Collecting urine samples
5. Measure and monitor catheter-associated urinary tract infection prevention processes and outcomes in high-volume areas by doing the following:

Chapter 5 | Prevent Health Care–Associated Infections

> **National Patient Safety Goal 7** *continued*
>
> - Selecting measures using evidence-based guidelines or best practices
> - Having a consistent method for medical record documentation of indwelling urinary catheter use, insertion, and maintenance
> - Monitoring compliance with evidence-based guidelines or best practices
> - Evaluating the effectiveness of prevention efforts

Central line–associated bloodstream infections (CLABSIs): A CLABSI is a serious infection that occurs when germs (usually bacteria or viruses) enter the bloodstream through the central line. These infections are preventable with education on proper catheter insertion and use. CLABSI is covered in NPSG.07.04.01 (*see* the "National Patient Safety Goal 7" sidebar).

Surgical site infections (SSIs): An SSI is an infection that occurs after surgery in the part of the body where the surgery took place. SSIs can be superficial infections that involve only the skin, or they can be more serious infections that involve tissues under the skin, deep tissues or organs, or implanted material. SSIs are a common problem. SSI is covered in NPSG.07.05.01.

Catheter-associated urinary tract infections (CAUTIs): CAUTI is an infection involving any part of the urinary system, including urethra, bladder, ureters, and kidney. It is the most common type of HAI infection reported to the National Healthcare Safety Network (NHSN), an arm of the US Centers for Disease Control and Prevention (CDC). To prevent CAUTI, it's vital to ensure catheters are used properly and for appropriate durations. CAUTI is covered in NPSG.07.06.01.

TRY THIS TOOL

CDC Checklist for CLABSI Prevention
This checklist from the US Centers for Disease Control and Prevention (CDC) can be used by clinicians and health care organizations to help prevent infections from central line–associated bloodstream infections. Visit the CDC's CLABSI resource page at https://www.cdc.gov/hai/bsi/bsi.html for additional resources.

99

Center for Transforming Healthcare
Surgical Site Infection Project

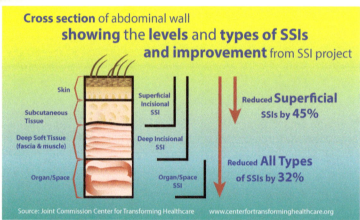

In a 2002 study of US hospitals, the estimated number of healthcare-associated infections (HAIs) was approximately 1.7 million. Surgical site infections (SSIs) were the second most common HAI, accounting for 22 percent of all HAIs among hospital patients. The estimated deaths associated with HAIs were 98,987, of which 8,205 (8 percent) were associated with SSIs.*

The SSI project began in August 2010 and was launched in collaboration with the American College of Surgeons (ACS) and seven participating organizations. The project uses SSI outcomes data derived from ACS's National Surgical Quality Improvement Program (NSQIP) to guide the improvement effort. NSQIP data on outcomes of surgery are highly regarded by physicians as clinically valid, using detailed medical information on severity of illness and comorbidity to produce data on risk-adjusted outcomes.

Colorectal surgery was identified as the focus of the project because it is a common procedure across different types of hospitals, can have significant complications, presents substantial opportunities for improvement, and has high variability in performance across hospitals. Project participants studied the potential factors that contribute to colorectal SSIs. There are three types of colorectal SSIs:

- Superficial incisional SSI – the infection involves only skin or subcutaneous tissue of the incision
- Deep incisional SSI – the infection appears to be related to the operation and involves deep soft tissues (for example, fascial and muscle layers) of the incision
- Organ/space SSI – the infection appears to be related to the operation and involves any part of the anatomy other than the incision (for example, organs or spaces), which was opened or manipulated during an operation

Project results

In November 2012, the Joint Commission Center for Transforming Healthcare announced solutions and findings for its fourth improvement project on reducing the risk of colorectal SSIs. Working together, the participating hospitals reduced superficial incisional colorectal SSIs by 45 percent and all types of colorectal SSIs by 32 percent. They attained an estimated cost savings of more than $3.7 million for the 135 estimated colorectal SSIs that were avoided. They also decreased the average length of stay for hospital patients with any type of colorectal SSI from 15 days to 13 days. In comparison, patients with no colorectal SSI had an average length of stay of eight days.

For more information on this project, its results, or the project participants visit the Center for Transforming Healthcare website.

* Sources of data:
Klevens RM, Edwards JR, et al: Estimating health care-associated infections and deaths in U.S. hospitals, 2002, *Public Health Reports 2007*;122:160-166

Emori TG, Gaynes RP: An overview of nosocomial infections, including the role of the microbiology laboratory, *Clinical Microbiology Reviews*, 1993:6(4):428-42

Chapter 5 | Prevent Health Care–Associated Infections

KEY CONCEPT
Risk Assessment

Now that you know more about the requirements for preventing infections, you'll need to put that guidance into action. You start by performing risk assessments on the areas we've discussed above. Here are some strategies for each type of HAI described at the beginning of the chapter:

Risk assessment strategies:
- **Conduct a risk assessment for MDROs**
  - Periodically assess the occurrence of MDROs in patients, health care personnel, and the community.
  - Identify epidemiologically important MDROs.
  - Integrate MDRO risk assessment into the overall IC risk assessment or create a stand-alone document.
  - Document findings in the IC plan.
- **Conduct a risk assessment for CLABSI**
  - Periodically assess the occurrence of CLABSI to identify at-risk populations.
  - Integrate CLABSI risk assessment into the overall IC risk assessment or create a stand-alone document.
  - Document CLABSI risk assessment findings in the IC plan.
- **Conduct a risk assessment for SSI**
  - Periodically assess the health care organization's patient population, types of surgical procedures performed, and regulatory and reporting requirements for your state or country.
  - Assess the occurrence of SSI to identify at-risk populations.
  - Integrate SSI risk assessment into the overall IC risk assessment or create a stand-alone document.
  - Document SSI risk assessment findings in the IC plan.
- **Conduct a risk assessment for CAUTI**
  - Periodically assess the occurrence of CAUTI to identify at-risk populations.
  - Integrate CAUTI risk assessment into the overall IC risk assessment or create a stand-alone document.
  - Document CAUTI risk assessment findings in the IC plan

TRY THIS TOOL

Risk Assessment Checklist for Surgical Site Infections
This checklist includes questions to ask to ensure that all interventions have been implemented to reduce the risk of surgical site infections within your organization.

in other words

Risk assessment

In this case, risk assessment refers to a method for estimating health risks from exposure to various levels of a workplace hazard. Understanding how much exposure to a hazard poses health risks to workers is important to appropriately eliminate, control, and reduce those risks. The aim of a risk assessment is to answer three basic questions:

1. What can happen?
2. How likely is it to happen?
3. What are the consequences if it does happen?

When conducting a risk assessment, the organization should carefully examine processes to ensure that they are based on current science and consistent with industry guidelines, standards, and recommendations. There should also be a process to determine whether staff are following policies and procedures related to IC.

A helpful first step is to create an inventory of all care, treatment, and services that the organization provides. The risk assessment or IC team can also visit each area of the organization to familiarize themselves with their processes, needs, and patient population.

While conducting a risk assessment, staff should consider outcome data related to HAIs in the organization. International Standard PCI.6 requires organizations to use a risk-based approach to establish the focus of their HAI prevention and control programs. In addition, PCI.6.1 requires that organizations track infection risks, rates, and trends related to HAIs to reduce the risks of those infections. Such surveillance may include the answers to questions such as, How many HAIs were identified during the preceding 12 months? What types of infections were involved? What were the contributing factors to these infections? These types of questions can help guide your risk assessment. The organization's surveillance data should also be taken into account and benchmarked against national and regional trends. (*See* page 107 for additional information about surveillance.)

Chapter 5 | **Prevent Health Care–Associated Infections**

> ## Risk Assessment for Infection Prevention
>
> A risk assessment should address the following questions to properly analyze risk for an infection event at your facility:
> - What is the probability that a risk event will occur at your facility?
> - If it occurs, how severe will it be?
> - What magnitude of response will be required by your organization?
> - How prepared is your organization to respond, should the event occur?
> - How will the event affect the target populations at your facility (patients, residents, staff)?
> - What is the expected frequency of occurrence?
> - What is your organization's ability to discover or detect the event?
> - What is the leadership support for addressing the event?
> - How will the risk affect the financial status of your organization?
> - Will the risk affect the physical environment?
> - Are there regulations that mandate managing certain risks?
> - Will your accreditation status be influenced?

KEY CONCEPT

Staff Education

Staff education and organizational commitment to learning can have a huge impact on reducing or eliminating HAIs. Preventing infections relies on education that reinforces best practices or leads to behavioral changes across your organization. It's important that staff understands its roles in IC efforts. To achieve staff commitment to your IC program, and adherence to IC regulations, your organization must continually educate staff about the following:

- How infections are transmitted to patients and staff
- The role of staff in preventing and controlling infection transmission, including their role in providing leadership, direct care, or supportive services
- The ways staff can identify potential infection prevention problems and develop the strategies to address those problems

103

- Specific policies and procedures for staff to prevent transmission of infection to patients and other staff
- Processes for staff reporting of infections and related problems, including which information to report and where to report it
- How caregivers can preserve their own health and safety

Strategies for health care personnel education:
- Develop and implement education activities about HAIs, MDROs, and IC strategies based on risk assessment and surveillance findings.
- Provide education at the time of hire and annually thereafter, or more frequently as needed, based on risk assessment, turnover, or changes in the patient population.
- Conduct skills fairs or other educational events related to IC. Base topics covered on risk assessments, identified compliance issues, or organization IC goals.
- Evaluate the effectiveness of education by monitoring compliance with IC protocols and the occurrence of HAIs.

KEY CONCEPT

Patient and Family Education

Patients and their visitors can get infections in health care facilities in a variety of ways. Germs can be spread from patient to patient, from health care personnel to patients, or through the improper use of equipment. These infections can cause sickness, emotional and financial distress, medical complications, and even death. That's why educating and empowering patients and families is critical to decreasing HAIs. Your health care organization must dedicate efforts to improve patient hygiene and to help patients understand the critical importance of their role in preventive care. Here are some strategies to educate patients and their families about infection issues.

Chapter 5 | **Prevent Health Care—Associated Infections**

Strategies for patient and family education:

- Discuss the importance of hand washing and cleanliness to reduce infection with patients, family members, and visitors.
- Hang posters and other reminders to clean hands by sinks, in restrooms, and in other strategic locations.
- Encourage patients, residents, and families to speak up and ask health care personnel to clean their hands.
- Provide education about HAIs and IC strategies to patients; educate family members as needed.
- Provide educational pamphlets, videos, scripted discussions, or a combination of techniques, depending on the learning levels of patients and their families.

It is also critical to assess the patient's and family's comprehension of the material you provided. One effective way of doing this is the "teach back" method, in which the recipients of information repeat and explain the information they were provided to ensure accurate understanding.

picture THIS

Patient Poster on HAI Prevention

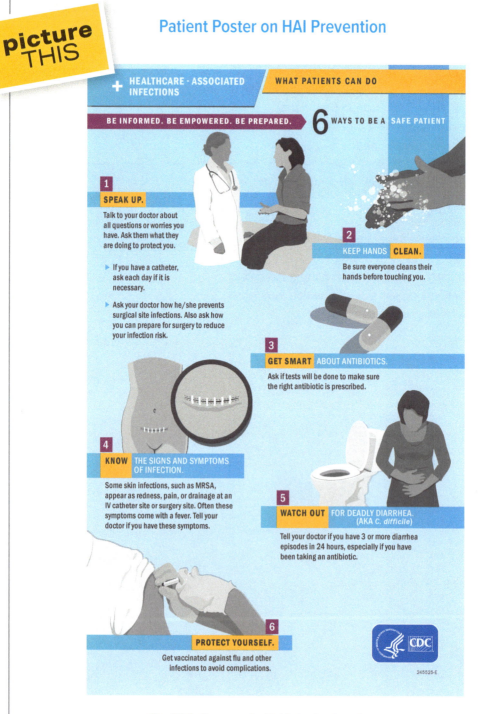

The CDC offers a poster that helps teach and empower patients on what they can do to help prevent HAIs.

Chapter 5 | **Prevent Health Care–Associated Infections**

KEY CONCEPT

Surveillance

Surveillance is a vital part of your IC program and essential to determining the best intervention strategies for HAIs. Surveillance involves collecting data about infections and practices. It will assist your organization in assessing infection risks for patients and staff, identifying areas that require further investigation, discovering new infections or outbreaks, and identifying the success of any changes made to a system or process. Surveillance data collection will also give you quantitative information about how well your IC program is helping to mitigate HAIs.

Assemble Your Team

To conduct effective surveillance, you should begin by assembling a team. Identify those leaders, managers, and others who can influence health care practices or provide technical support for data collection, management, and analysis. Then assemble a working group. Collaborate with the group members to develop the program, create a written plan for surveillance activities, implement the plan, and periodically evaluate the program.

Build Your Surveillance Program

The Joint Commission and JCI do not specify in their requirements how an organization should conduct surveillance, or what data organizations should collect. Consider tracking IC risks prevalent in your organization, as identified in your IC risk assessment. Organizations should also be familiar with any local, regional, or national laws or regulations that require reporting of certain data.

When designing your program, including the following components is a good rule of thumb (note that the examples included are not exhaustive but are emblematic of the types of data organizations may choose to track):

- Assess and define the population(s) to be monitored (for example, intensive care unit patients, pediatric patients, surgical patients, staff).
- Choose the events/indicators to be monitored. These could include process measures and/or outcome measures, such as the following examples:

107

- Process measures:
  - Influenza immunization rates in personnel, residents, or patients
  - Personnel compliance with hand hygiene, standard precautions, or other IC practice
- Outcome measures:
  - Device-associated infections, such as CLABSI or CAUTI
  - SSI following a specific operative procedure
  - Infection or colonization with a specific organism, such as methicillin-reisistant *Staphylococcus aureus* or *Clostridium difficile*
• Identify surveillance criteria/case definitions. For example, if you are tracking SSIs associated with heart surgeries in your organization, create a list of procedures for which you will be tracking data. Determine which types of patients and which types of procedures should be included.
• Determine the time period for observation (for example, track monthly data, quarterly data, or annual data).
• Determine methods for data collection, management, analysis, and reporting. Many methodologies exist. Organizations many want to consider these commonly used methods:
  - Create a database in which to enter data points (such as number of HAIs, number of sharps injuries, others selected by your organization).
  - Create a laboratory reporting system in which the lab notifies infection preventionists or other designated stakeholder when an HAI is detected in diagnostic testing.
  - Review medical records postdischarge for data relevant to the measures you selected.
  - Count HAIs, assess risk factors, and monitor patient care procedures.
  - Monitor patients for HAIs during their stay in the organization.
• Identify recipients of surveillance data and reports (for example, organization leaders, physicians, IC Committee).
• Use surveillance findings in quality assurance/performance improvement activities. For example, use trends identified through your surveillance process to establish and prioritize performance improvement goals.

Chapter 5 | Prevent Health Care–Associated Infections

KEY CONCEPT

Implement Evidence-Based Practices

Evidence-based practices are recommendations developed by professional health care organizations, government entities, or other groups that measure the quality of your IC practices. They provide a summary of tested strategies and techniques that can aid your organization in your efforts to reduce the risk of HAIs.

Evidenced-based guidelines are also required by The Joint Commission and JCI in their IC–related accreditation standards, NPSGs, and IPSGs. National Patient Safety Goal 7 requires health care programs to implement evidence-based practices to prevent MDRO infections in organizations, SSIs, CLABSIs, and CAUTIs, as discussed earlier in this chapter. And JCI Standard IPSG.5 requires the use of evidence-based hand hygiene guidelines to reduce HAIs.

With the exception of requiring use of the CDC or World Health Organization (WHO) evidenced-based guidelines for hand hygiene, The Joint Commission and JCI don't specify which guidelines organizations should adopt. Rather, they require organizations to adhere to the guidelines, policies, and proce-dures that they select.

One valuable resource when choosing guidelines for orga-nizations in the United States is the CDC's Guidelines Library. This online resource provides guidelines that address basic IC practices, as well as device- and procedure-associated IC guidelines, antibiotic resistance guidelines, infectious organism–specific guidelines, guidelines for worker safety, and other IC issues. Go to https://www.cdc.gov/infectioncontrol/guidelines/index.html to visit the library.

smart questions:

What evidence-based practices are being used to eliminate HAIs at your health care facility?

TOOLS OF THE TRADE

- Compliance Assessment Checklist for NPSG 7
- Risk Assessment Matrix for Prevention of MDROs
- CDC Checklist for CLABSI Prevention
- Risk Assessment Checklist for Surgical Site Infections

Additional Resources

Joint Commission Infection Prevention and Control Portal
The Joint Commission's Infection Prevention and Control portal offers information on key IC issues, as well as resources from The Joint Commission, Joint Commission Resources, and the Joint Commission Center for Transforming Healthcare. Visit the portal at https://www.jointcommission.org/hai.aspx.

CLABSI Resource Page
The CDC provides guidelines and tools to the health care community to help end CLABSIs. Visit the CLABSI resource page at https://www.cdc.gov/hai/bsi/bsi.html.

CAUTI Resource Page
The CDC, in collaboration with other organizations, has developed guidelines for the prevention of catheter-associated UTIs and other types of HAIs. Visit the resource page: https://www.cdc.gov/hai/ca_uti/uti.html.

World Health Organization
WHO also offers evidence-based guidelines for national and acute health care facility IC efforts. Visit http://www.who.int/gpsc/ipc-components/en/ to view these guidelines. Ministries of health and other agencies in many countries have developed their own guidelines. For example, the European Centre for Disease Prevention and Control and the Chinese Centers for Disease Control and Prevention have developed a number of IC guidelines.

Chapter 5 | **Prevent Health Care–Associated Infections**

The Compendium

In addition to government and WHO resources, you may choose to consult a professional organization such as the Society for Healthcare Epidemiology of America (SHEA) or the Association for Professionals in Infection Control and Epidemiology (APIC). A number of these organizations, including The Joint Commission, SHEA, APIC, and others, collaborated in 2008 to develop *A Compendium of Strategies to Prevent Healthcare-Associated Infections in Acute Care Hospitals*. The compendium, which was updated in 2014, provides acute care hospitals with up-to-date, practical, expert guidance to assist in prioritizing and implementing their HAI prevention efforts. The compendium is available at https://www.ncbi.nlm.nih.gov/pmc/articles/PMC4223864/.

CHAPTER 6

Provide Safe Medical Equipment, Devices, and Supplies

The US Centers for Disease Control and Prevention (CDC) estimates that 46.5 million surgical procedures are performed in hospitals and ambulatory settings each year, including approximately 5 million gastrointestinal endoscopies.

Each of these procedures involves contact with a medical device or surgical instrument, which poses a major risk of introducing pathogens that can lead to infection. Even more people are at risk of developing an infection from contact with medical equipment, devices, or supplies while seeking other health services. That is why it's vital to properly clean, disinfect, sterilize, and store medical equipment, devices, and supplies. There are numerous steps involved in these processes that are designed to minimize infection risks and transmission. Health care workers need to follow standardized practices to maintain a reliable system.

Surgery Around the World

Currently no data are available on the number of surgeries that are performed globally. However, the World Bank provides country-by-country data at this website: https://data.worldbank.org/indicator/SH.SGR.PROC.P5?view=chart. Click on the name of each country in the list to see the data for that location. Note that some countries did not report data.

KEY CONCEPTS

- Categorization of Items to Be Reprocessed Based on Infection Risk
- Common Risks Associated with Cleaning, Disinfection, and Sterilization Failures
- Strategies for Preventing or Mitigating Risk

KEY CONCEPT

Categorization of Items to Be Reprocessed Based on Infection Risk

Reprocessing means subjecting medical instruments to a special process or treatment in preparation for reuse, so the tools are completely disinfected and sterilized. The most common approach to disinfection and sterilization was developed by Earle Spaulding, MD, in 1957. The Spaulding Classification defines the minimum levels of disinfection or sterilization required for the three different categories of medical devices based on intended use. The system classifies medical devices to be reprocessed as critical, semicritical, and noncritical according to the following risk infections. Table 6-1 summarizes how items should be reprocessed based on the risk of infection for the patient based on the Spaulding Classification.

Critical items: Items such as surgical instruments, cardiac catheters, implants, and invasive catheters that enter the vascular system or contact sterile tissues or fluids are categorized as *critical*. These items create a high risk of infection and require sterilization.

Semicritical items: Items such as medical instrument blades and respiratory therapy equipment that contact mucous membranes (eyes, mouth, nose, vagina, gastrointestinal tract) and nonintact skin are categorized as *semicritical*. These items require at least high-level disinfection. (*See* pages 115-116 for an explanation of the differences between cleaning, decontamination, disinfection, and sterilization.)

in other words

Item reprocessing

This term refers to the process of cleaning, disinfecting, and sterilizing medical instruments in preparation for reuse.

 **TRY THIS TOOL**

Evaluation of Item for Reprocessing Form

This form can be used to assess your organization's reprocessing procedures.

Chapter 6 | **Provide Safe Medical Equipment, Devices, and Supplies**

Noncritical items: Items that contact intact skin, but not secretion membranes, are categorized as *noncritical*. They require cleaning with or without low- or intermediate-level disinfection, depending on intended use.

Table 6-1. Categorization of Items to Be Reprocessed Based on Risk of Infection*

Level	Risk of Infection	Description	Examples of Items	Reprocessing Methods
Critical	High	Item comes in contact with or enters sterile tissue, sterile body cavity, or the vascular system	Surgical and dental instruments, inner surfaces of hemodialyzers, urinary catheters, biopsy forceps, implants, intravascular devices, and needles	Sterilization
Semicritical	Moderate	Item comes in contact with mucous membrane or non-intact skin	Respiratory therapy and anesthesia equipment, some endoscopes, laryngoscope blades, esophageal manometry probes, vaginal ultrasound probes and specula, and diaphragm fitting rings	Minimum: High-level disinfection (when practical, sterilization preferred)
Noncritical	Low	Item comes in contact intact skin	Patient care Items: bedpans, blood pressure cuffs, crutches, incubators, and computers Environmental surfaces: bed rails, bedside tables, patient furniture, counters, and floor	Low and intermediate disinfection

* This table follows the Spaulding Classification, a widely used strategy for sterilization or disinfection of inanimate objects and surfaces based on the degree of risk involved in their use.

Four basic types of processing will remove pathogens, dirt, and debris from equipment. The type of processing depends on the type of equipment processed.

Reprocessing types
- **Cleaning:** Removes all visible dust, soil, and any other visible material that microorganisms might find favorable for continued life and growth. This is usually done by scrubbing with hot water and detergent. Precleaning is performed for some instruments, for example in the operating room following the surgical procedure. The precleaning makes it easier for the sterile processing staff to effectively clean the instruments when they arrive at that department.
- **Decontamination:** Removes disease-producing organisms, rendering equipment safe to handle.

115

- **Disinfection:** Destroys most disease-producing organisms but not all microbial forms. There are three levels of disinfection:
  1. High level—kills all organisms except high levels of bacterial spores
  2. Intermediate level—kills mycobacteria, most viruses, and bacteria
  3. Low level—kills some viruses and bacteria
- **Sterilization:** Destroys all forms of microbial life, including bacteria, viruses, spores, and fungi.

KEY CONCEPT

Common Risks Associated with Cleaning, Disinfection, and Sterilization Failures

Deficiencies in the cleaning, disinfection, and sterilization of medical devices, equipment, and supplies can leave infectious material on these items, which can potentially cause health care–associated infections (HAIs), outbreaks of infection, and harm to patients. Inadequate reprocessing can also result in other adverse patient outcomes, such as tissue irritation from residual reprocessing materials, for example, from chemical disinfectants. It's vital to reduce the risk of infection with each step of cleaning, disinfection, and sterilization. If health care staff at your organization improperly clean, disinfect, and sterilize instruments, common risks for transmission of infection may include the following:

- Inconsistent reprocessing of the instrument or equipment
- Failure to follow standard reprocessing procedures
- Failure to follow manufacturer's instructions for use
- Inadequate or ineffective manufacturer's instructions for use
- Use of expired detergents or disinfectants
- Design flaws in the device or equipment
- Continued use of devices despite integrity, maintenance, and mechanical issues
- Lack of adequate training and competency of personnel responsible for using or reprocessing medical devices and equipment

Chapter 6 | Provide Safe Medical Equipment, Devices, and Supplies

Frontline staff should also know to whom they should report IC concerns, including those related to cleaning, disinfection, or sterilization. For example, if a nurse notices that items that should be kept sterile have damaged packaging that could lead to contamination, he or she should have a means of notifying those responsible for processing that equipment or the organization's infection preventionist(s).

smart questions:

Is your facility adhering to manufacturers' guidelines when cleaning, disinfecting, or sterilizing medical equipment, devices, and supplies?

KEY CONCEPT

Strategies for Preventing or Mitigating Risk

Guidelines and Best Practices

In general, HAIs can be prevented if your organization follows these basic guidelines when performing cleaning, disinfection, and sterilization:

- Use instruments as intended by the manufacturers.
- Explicitly follow manufacturer's instructions.
- Implement clear policies and procedures for use and processing that include evidence-based infection prevention and control (IC) practices.
- Implement stringent quality controls on use and reprocessing.
- Ensure that staff are trained and competent to reprocess each instrument or medical device.
- Provide appropriate space, supplies, and equipment to support use and reprocessing.
- Maintain standardization of processes regardless of whether it is performed in one central location or department or in different areas throughout the organization.
- Continually assess your organization's reprocessing program to identify any factors that may contribute to risk and implement improvement strategies.
- Reinforce the process by emphasizing to staff that failure to perform any of the steps in reprocessing can lead to infection and other risks.
- Periodically assess staff competency of those responsible for cleaning, disinfecting, and sterilizing equipment.
- Provide refresher training for staff at regular intervals to maintain competency.

- Review reprocessing procedures to ensure that they are comprehensive and easily accessible to staff who engage in cleaning, disinfection, and sterilization, and to ensure that your program is in compliance with current standards.
- Confirm that reprocessing procedures are aligned with current manufacturer recommendations for cleaning.
- Invite input from staff when assessing new instruments or equipment that require reprocessing, such as surgical instruments, endocavity probes, and other items.
- Keep lines of communication open between reprocessing staff and the clinical departments they support.

smart questions:

Are relevant and current references for cleaning, disinfection, and sterilization of medical devices and equipment accessible to those who need them? How does your organization ensure that recommended practices are implemented effectively?

Guidelines and practices to help meet requirements of Standard IC.02.02.01:

The Joint Commission Infection Prevention and Control (IC) Standard IC.02.02.01 requires your organization to reduce the risk of infections associated with medical equipment, devices, and supplies. As we've discussed, there is a real risk for patients to develop an infection, or person-to-person transmission of infections, if staff fail to properly prepare items for reuse. A similar Joint Commission International (JCI) requirement for international organizations at Prevention and Control of Infections (PCI) Standard PCI.7: The organization reduces the risk of infections associated with medical/surgical equipment, devices, and supplies by ensuring adequate cleaning, disinfection, sterilization, and storage; and implements a process for managing expired supplies.

There are numerous steps involved in these processes, so it is critical that reprocessing staff follow standardized practices. To maintain a reliable system for controlling this process, organizations must pay attention to the following:

- Orientation, training, and competency of health care workers who are processing medical equipment, devices, and supplies
- Levels of staffing and supervision of the health care workers who are processing medical equipment, devices, and supplies
- Adequate well-functioning equipment to support best practices

Chapter 6 | Provide Safe Medical Equipment, Devices, and Supplies

- Standardization of process regardless of whether it is centralized or decentralized

There are a variety of standardized guidelines by organizations that can assist your IC team in implementing best practices. Consider the following examples:

- **AAMI standards:** The Association for the Advancement of Medical Instrumentation (AAMI) offers several comprehensive guides:
  - **ST41—Ethylene Oxide Sterilization in Health Care Facilities:** Safety and Effectiveness (2018). This recommended practice covers the safe and effective use of ethylene oxide as a sterilant in health care facilities. This guideline can help organizations ensure sterility while also limiting staff exposure to associated chemicals.
  - **ST91—Flexible and Semi-Rigid Endoscope Processing in Health Care Facilities (2015).** Provides guidelines for health care personnel in precleaning, leak-testing, cleaning, packaging, storage, high-level disinfecting, and/or sterilizing of equipment used to examine the digestive and respiratory systems. These include items such as endoscopes and semi-rigid operative endoscopes in health care facilities.
  - **ST58—Chemical Sterilization and High-Level Disinfection in Health Care Facilities (2013).** This standard provides guidelines for the selection and use of liquid and gaseous materials that can be used in cleaning, disinfection, and sterilization. The guideline also addresses design of areas used for these purposes, as well as staff qualifications and safety issues.
- **CDC guidelines:** The CDC offers a variety of guidelines and updates for disinfection and sterilization and environmental infection control:
  - **Guidelines for Disinfection and Sterilization in Healthcare Facilities, 2008** https://www.cdc.gov/infectioncontrol/guidelines/disinfection/index.html
  - **Guidelines for Environmental Infection Control in Health-Care Facilities, 2003** https://www.cdc.gov/infectioncontrol/guidelines/environmental/index.html

119

- **CMS *State Operations Manual*:** The US Centers for Medicare & Medicaid Services (CMS) offers two worksheets to help you with assessments in infection control:
  - **Ambulatory Surgical Center (ASC) Infection Control Surveyor Worksheet**
  - https://www.cms.gov/Regulations-and-Guidance/Guidance/Manuals/downloads/som107_exhibit_351.pdf
  - **Hospital Infection Control Worksheet**
  - https://www.cms.gov/Medicare/Provider-Enrollment-and-Certification/SurveyCertificationGenInfo/Downloads/Survey-and-Cert-Letter-15-12-Attachment-1.pdf
- **FDA Medical Devices Section:** The US Food and Drug Administration (FDA) has a webpage dedicated to guidance on medical devices at http://www.fda.gov/MedicalDevices/default.htm. It includes information on the following:
  - **Products and Medical Procedures**—Approvals & Clearances; Home Use; Surgical, Implants & Prosthetics; In Vitro Diagnostics; and so forth
  - **Medical Device Safety**—Alerts & Notices, Recalls, Report a Problem, MedSun, Emergency Situations
  - **Device Advice: Comprehensive Regulatory Assistance**—Device Advice, FDA's Center for Devices and Radiological Health (CDRH) webpage for comprehensive regulatory education
  - **Digital Health**—Information about CDRH's Digital Health Program
  - **Science and Research (Medical Devices)**—Science at CDRH includes laboratory and field research in the areas of physical, life, and engineering sciences as well as epidemiological research in postmarket device safety.
  - **International Programs**—International Medical Device Regulators Forum, Medical Device Single Audit Program Pilot
  - **News & Events (Medical Devices)**—Medical Device News, Videos, Workshops & Meetings
  - **Resources for You (Medical Devices)**—Information of special interest to specific audiences and stakeholders
- **Facility Guidelines Institute:** The Facility Guidelines Institute (FGI) offers guidelines for purchase at https://www.fgiguidelines.org/guidelines/purchase-the-guidelines/ that

Chapter 6 | Provide Safe Medical Equipment, Devices, and Supplies

include help with IC and other relevant topics related to medical equipment:
- 2018 *Guidelines for Design and Construction of Hospitals*
- 2018 *Guidelines for Design and Construction of Outpatient Facilities*

• **World Health Organization:** The World Health Organization (WHO) offers guidance on cleaning, disinfection, and sterilization in a document titled *Decontamination and Reprocessing of Medical Devices for Health-care Facilities*, available at http://apps.who.int/iris/bitstream/handle/10665/250232/9789241549851-eng.

Manufacturers' Guidelines

Adherence to manufacturers' instructions for the devices and equipment used in your facility is critical, as are the products needed to reprocess them properly. Always follow the manufacturer's recommended or required cleaning, disinfection, or sterilization instructions for the device before purchasing. You want to know if the instruments can be processed, what cleansers or disinfectants are required to keep them clean and disinfected, and if the required cleaning agents are readily available. This can help ensure that the product will be processed and that the compatible cleansers or disinfectants are available.

TRY THIS TOOL

Steps for Assessing Reprocessing of Instruments, Equipment, and Supplies
This tool can be used for a step-by-step process for following manufacturer's guidelines for reprocessing instruments and equipment.

Tips for Cleaning Commonly Used Items

To meet the requirements for cleaning commonly used and noncritical devices, your organization will need to implement procedures that adhere to manufacturers' guidelines. Table 6-2 on page 122 offers a sample chart for tracking the cleaning of frequently used equipment and devices. Such a chart may include the item description, the job role responsible for cleaning the item, the product(s) that should be used to clean the item, and the frequency of cleaning, for example. Start by answering the following questions:
• Who is responsible for cleaning and disinfecting items?
• Which equipment and supplies can be cleaned and reused? Which are disposable?

121

- What cleaning and disinfecting products should be used?
- Where should cleaning and disinfecting efforts occur?
- When should equipment and supplies be cleaned?
- How should cleaning and disinfecting be done?
- What disposable equipment can never be reused?
- Who will monitor and keep the records of reprocessing?

Table 6-2. Guidelines for Cleaning Frequently Used Equipment

Item	Location	Role Responsible for Cleaning	Frequency of Cleaning	Product Used to Clean	Comments
Blood Pressure Machine	Clinics	Person Using Machine (for example, medical assistant, nurse, MD)	After Every Patient Use	Pop-Up Wipe (specify compatible product name)	
Blood Pressure Machine	Inpatient Units—Portable	Person Using Machine (for example, nursing assistant, nurse)	After Every Patient Use	XYZ Wipes	
Blood Pressure Machine	Pre- and Postprocedure Units	Person Using Machine (for example, nurse, anesthesiologist)	After Every Patient Use	XYZ Wipes	
Installed Monitors	Inpatient Units	Environmental Services (EVS)	After Each Discharge	XYZ Wipes	Special Instructions: Do not use disinfect wipe on screen; wipe screen with clean cloth.
Pill Crusher	Medication Rooms	EVS	Every Friday 1st Shift	Soap and Water	
Procedure Table—Radiology	Scanning Rooms	Radiology Tech (RT)	Patient Surface After Every Patient (RT) Entire Table Every Friday Evening Shift (EVS)	ABC Disinfectant	EVS Worker Must Be Trained on Specific Table Cleaning Instructions (for example, control panel)

Equipment should be cleaned and disinfected before and after each patient use, and when it passes from department to department. All equipment should undergo decontamination before being transported to an equipment maintenance department, and then again before going to a direct-use environment.

Manufacturers of equipment must provide cleaning, disinfection, and sterilization instructions. If guidelines are not provided, you must contact the company and request them. If they cannot or will not provide the instructions, consider not using the instrument, device, or equipment.

Chapter 6 | Provide Safe Medical Equipment, Devices, and Supplies

Staff must have the proper space to perform cleaning, disinfecting, and sterilization in order. The space should be built to standards that protect staff and equipment and minimize any risk of cross-contamination. Barriers between the dirty areas and clean areas, for example, are recommended.

Personal protective equipment (PPE) should be available to staff to prevent biological and chemical exposure, and it should be easy to use so that cleanliness in the space is managed properly. Resources for hand hygiene should be provided as well.

Tips for High-Level Disinfection

As discussed earlier, medical devices categorized as semicritical according to the Spaulding Classification, such as medical instrument blades, endoscopes, and respiratory therapy equipment, require at least high-level disinfection. This level of cleaning is also mandated by Joint Commission Standard IC.02.02.01, Element of Performance (EP) 2—an organization implements infection prevention and control activities when doing the following: Performing intermediate and high-level disinfection and sterilization of medical equipment, devices, and supplies.

Proper high-level disinfection of medical devices requires staff to do the following:
- Identify all medical devices and equipment used in the facility.
- Identify devices that require high-level disinfection or sterilization, and the areas where they are used and reprocessed.
- Ensure that manufacturer's cleaning and disinfection instructions for each item are readily available to staff performing reprocessing procedures.
- Ensure that the correct environment, equipment, and supplies are available to reprocess a device, per manufacturer's instructions.
- Develop and implement policies and procedures for disinfection and sterilization, including use of PPE in accordance with manufacturers' instructions for use, evidence-based practices, and regulatory requirements.

123

- Implement reprocessing training and testing programs to ensure competence of all personnel who reprocess medical devices and equipment.
- Offer training of personnel in the correct use, donning, removal, limitations, and indications for PPE to prevent biological and/or chemical exposure.
- Ensure consistent quality control and documentation in all areas performing high-level disinfection and sterilization so that the processes can be audited for compliance.
- Follow the recommended dilution of cleaning chemicals and soak times. Test the dilution before each procedure.
- Use signage to indicate how much product is added to a specified amount of water, if an automated dilution system is not used.
- Perform periodic validation of systems that automate dilution of cleaning chemicals as recommended by the manufacturer.
- Rinse items according to the manufacturer's instructions for using the cleaning agent.
- Brush all instruments underwater to prevent aerosolization during cleaning. Brushes must be the correct diameter, length, bristle type, and material for the instrument or equipment to be cleaned.
- Follow manufacturer's instructions to ensure that the correct brush is used. Brushes are labeled as single- or multiple-use items and should be used accordingly.
- Disinfect or sterilize any reusable brushes at least daily, in accordance with manufacturer's instructions.

Chapter 6 | Provide Safe Medical Equipment, Devices, and Supplies

Key Areas Requiring High-Level Disinfection

Key areas where devices requiring high-level disinfection can be found include the following:

- Emergency department: Endoscopes, endocavity probes (such as vaginal or rectal probes)
- OB/GYN clinic: Endocavity probe, diaphragm fitting rings
- Sleep study units: Reusable sleep study masks and tubing
- Gastroenterology or pulmonary procedure units and clinics: Colonoscopes, duodenoscopes, bronchoscopes
- ICUs: Endoscopes, transesophageal echocardiography probes
- Radiology: Endocavity probes
- Urology clinic: Endoscopes, endocavity probes
- Operating and procedure rooms and sterile processing: Endoscopes, transesophageal echocardiography probes
- Ambulatory surgery centers, office-based surgery practice: Endoscopes, laryngoscopes
- Cardiac procedure areas: Transesophageal echocardiography probes

Tips for Sterilization

To prevent patients from being infected with disease, you must sterilize medical equipment properly. Sterilization prevents the buildup of bacteria on tools and prevents the spread of diseases to other patients. If an infection is caused by unsterile equipment, a second surgery may be needed. An infection may not manifest right away, but if it does it can be life-threatening.

To avoid these complications and keep patients safe, make sure all instruments are properly sterilized. Here are some steps to follow:

Precleaning: Clean instruments at point of use, such as the procedure room, by flushing lumens with sterile water and wiping off any tissue or blood with a moistened sponge during the procedure. If instruments aren't transported to reprocessing right away, cover them with an enzymatic spray, gel, or foam, compatible detergent, or a cloth moistened with water to prevent drying. Follow the manufacturer's product instructions.

smart questions:

Have reprocessing staff been trained on the proper use of PPE to prevent biological or chemical exposure during disinfection and sterilization?

Transport items to reprocessing: Place contaminated instruments in a closed, leak-proof container. For sharp instruments, use a puncture-resistant, leak-proof, container that meets US Occupational Safety and Health Administration (OSHA) standards, and label it. Place a biohazard label on the transport container of soiled items. After items are contained, take them to the reprocessing area.

Reprocessing procedures: There are a number of steps to take when sterilizing instruments in the reprocessing area:

Disassemble instruments: Take apart instruments, as specified by the instrument manufacturer's instructions, during the cleaning and sterilization process.

Clean instruments before sterilization: Thorough cleaning is required to remove all organic matter to ensure that the sterilant can reach the surfaces of the items processed.

Process instruments immediately: Items should be processed as soon as possible. Do not let them sit overnight.

Rinse instruments: Follow the specific instructions for rinsing that come with cleaning or disinfection chemicals.

Dry instruments: Read the manufacturer's instructions on drying instruments during reprocessing steps. This will vary. Items should be completely dry before placed in storage.

Inspect instruments: All instruments should be inspected for missed grime or damage during and after the cleaning process. If damaged, set aside for repair, or discard.

Lubricate instruments: Some instruments may require lubrication to keep the moving parts from sticking, and to prevent corrosion.

Select proper containers and wrapping: The containers you use must be certified for use with the sterilization process. Take care when using wrapping supplies by following manufacturer's instructions.

Select the proper sterilant: The sterilant you use must adhere to the manufacturer's instructions for the instrument and the sterilizer.

Chapter 6 | Provide Safe Medical Equipment, Devices, and Supplies

Monitor sterilization: Monitor the sterilization process by using chemical, biological, and physical indicators as outlined by the manufacturer.

- Chemical indicators include the color-changing strips placed within the sterilization container after processing. Follow container manufacturer's instructions for where indicators should be placed. Make sure staff know what color changes are expected for the indicator. Each indicator is different.
- Biological indicators should be included in at least one sterilizer load per week and every load that includes an implant. The results of biologic indicators require documentation.
- Physical indicators include time, temperature, and pressure, which must be monitored per sterilizer manufacturer's instructions.

Verify the sterilization process: For quality-control purposes, verification that the sterilization procedures were done correctly should be required before removing an item from the sterilizer.

Label instruments and trays: From the time of sterilization until use, a label must be affixed to the contained item or tray so that it can be tracked. The label should include what the contents are, and the date they were sterilized, along with an identifier that allows tracking.

The infection preventionist should work closely with sterile processing staff to ensure that sterilization and high-level disinfection processes are performed correctly and consistently among all areas involved with medical device cleaning, disinfection, and sterilization.

Maintenance and testing of sterilizers: Joint Commission Environment of Care (EC) Standard EC.02.04.03, EP 4, requires your organization to maintain sterilizers, conduct performance testing on them, and document those activities. The sterilization process, including equipment used to sterilize devices, must work effectively to ensure patient safety. To comply with this standard, your organization must provide documentation showing that your sterilizer performance testing (including physical, chemical, and biological monitoring) and maintenance are performed in accordance with standardized, accepted practices, and manufacturer's guidelines.

International organizations must comply with JCI Facility Management and Safety (FMS) Standard FMS.8: The organization establishes a program for inspecting, testing, and maintaining medical equipment and documenting the results. This includes implementing an organizationwide medical equipment program, creating an inventory of all medical equipment, conducting inspections and tests of equipment, staff training, and preventive maintenance.

COLLABORATION: Infection preventionists should collaborate with staff who use sterilizers to review maintenance and performance to ensure that the sterilization process is being followed and equipment is working properly.

Additional strategies for compliance: Your organization must comply with several additional requirements that involve cleaning, disinfecting, and sterilizing medical instruments. These are discussed below.

- **IC.02.02.01, EP 3:** Implement infection prevention and control activities when doing the following: Disposing of medical equipment, devices, and supplies.
- **PCI.7.2 (International only):** The organization reduces the risk of infections through proper disposal of waste.
- **PCI.7.3 (International only):** The organization implements practices for the safe handling and disposal of sharps and needles.

How to Comply

Make sure staff dispose of used medical equipment, devices, and supplies according to federal, state, and local requirements. The rules for managing hazardous waste varies from state to state, but in general, you'll need to segregate infectious medical waste from regular waste. Any infectious waste will need to be packaged properly according to requirements for transportation and disposal sites. Transparent procedures to meet these requirements must be established, and staff education on disposal policies should be a priority.

- **IC.02.02.01, EP 4:** Implement infection prevention and control activities when doing the following: Storing medical equipment, devices, and supplies.

Chapter 6 | Provide Safe Medical Equipment, Devices, and Supplies

- **PCI.7, Measureable Element (ME) 5 (International only):** Clean and sterile supplies are properly stored in designated storage areas that are clean and dry and protected from dust, moisture, and temperature extremes.

How to Comply

Store supplies in protected areas and regulate access to them. Common IC problems related to storage include the following:

- Failure to comply with manufacturers' instructions for storing equipment, devices, and supplies
- Failure to comply with local, state, or federal rules or regulations
- Failure to comply with Joint Commission standards or evidence-based guidelines
- Failure to comply with organization policies and procedures
- Failure to separate clean and soiled or contaminated items, or storing clean items in an insufficiently clean location

Health care organizations must follow manufacturer's instructions for use, including care and storage of the item. For example, if the manufacturer's instructions states "Do not store in the original shipping container," or "Store between 2°C to 8°C," the expectation of The Joint Commission and JCI is that those instructions are followed.

Complying with law and regulation is another important component of safe storage. Most countries and US states have slightly different requirements, and facilities must familiarize themselves with the requirements of their state and local government.

In the absence of manufacturer's instructions or regulations, facilities can develop policies requiring adherence to a particular set of evidence-based standards or guidelines they are following; for example, the Association of periOperative Registered Nurses (AORN) Guidelines for Sterile Technique, or the AAMI steam sterilization standard ST79:2017.

- **IC.02.02.01, EP 5:** When reprocessing single-use devices, implement infection prevention and control activities that are consistent with regulatory and professional standards.

- **PCI.7.1 (International only):** The organization identifies and implements a process for managing the reuse of single-use devices consistent with regional and local laws and regulations.

How to Comply

Inappropriate reprocessing of single-use devices (SUDs) can compromise patient safety. The FDA has strict requirements for reprocessing devices labeled for single use under the Federal Food, Drug, and Cosmetic Act. SUDs should not be reprocessed and reused unless your organization can meet the FDA or JCI requirements. If you cannot meet them, you will need to obtain a third-party reprocessor that can, or simply choose not to reprocess and reuse SUDs. Make sure there is a clearly written policy regarding SUDs and reprocessing. For more information on FDA regulations regarding SUDs visit https://www.federalregister.gov/documents/2005/09/29/05-19510/medical-devices-reprocessed-single-use-devices-termination-of-exemptions-from-premarket-notification#h-14.

WHO's regulations for medical devices also contain guidance related to SUDs. Review those documents here: http://www.who.int/medical_devices/publications/en/MD_Regulations.pdf.

> **⬇ TRY THIS TOOL**
>
> **Sample Endoscope Inventory Form**
> This tool can be used to track endoscopes that are taken in and out of service.

Chapter 6 | **Provide Safe Medical Equipment, Devices, and Supplies**

Endoscopes

Endoscopes, devices that can be introduced into the body to view its internal parts, are medical devices commonly linked to infectious outbreaks. They pose a high risk due to high levels of bacterial contamination. Endoscopes require low-temperature sterilization or disinfection methods, and their design poses substantial challenges to reprocessing.

Endoscopes should be initially cleaned next to the exam table or bed with an enzymatic detergent or other cleaner or water as recommended by the manufacturer. This process is known as precleaning and is typically done with a brush or sponge. PPE recommended by the manufacturer while performing precleaning should be used. Note that precleaning is not the thorough cleaning required before disinfection.

After precleaning has been performed, the endoscope should be taken to a reprocessing area in a leakproof, puncture-resistant container. It should also be labeled as biohazardous. Reprocessing of endoscopes includes the following:

- Leak testing
- Manual cleaning
- Rinse after cleaning
- Visual inspection
- High-level disinfection (manual or automated)
- Rinse after high-level disinfection
- Drying (alcohol and forced air)

All endoscopes must be trackable, so it's important to create a master list of all endoscopes available in your facility.

TOOLS OF THE TRADE

- Evaluation of Item for Reprocessing Form
- Steps for Assessing Reprocessing of Instruments, Equipment, and Supplies
- Sample Endoscope Inventory Form

CHAPTER 7

Manage Infection Prevention and Control in the Environment of Care

Activities such as maintaining your utility systems—such as water systems and heat, ventilating, and air-conditioning (HVAC) systems—are an important part of an infection prevention and control (IC) plan. Failing to keep your utility systems running properly can create infection risk or increase the chances of it developing. Poorly maintained utilities may also spread airborne pathogens through badly serviced or malfunctioning HVAC systems.

Infection risks may also develop when the environment of care is disrupted due to demolition, renovation, or construction. To help ensure that the utilities in your facility are not spreading infection, your organization is required by The Joint Commission Environment of Care (EC) standards to do the following:
- Manage risks associated with utilities (EC.02.05.01).
- Establish and maintain a safe, functional environment (EC.02.06.01).
- Manage your environment during demolition, renovation, or new construction to reduce risk to those in the organization (EC.02.06.05).

Organizations accredited by Joint Commission International (JCI) must meet the following requirements in the Facility Management and Safety (FMS) and Prevention and Control of Infections (PCI) standards:

- Establish and implement a program to ensure that all utility systems operate effectively and efficiently (FMS.9).
- Plan and implement a program to provide a safe physical facility through inspection and planning to reduce risks (FMS.4).
- When planning for demolition, construction, or renovation, the organization conducts a preconstruction risk assessment (FMS.4.2.1).
- Reduce the risk of infection associated with mechanical and engineering controls and during demolition, construction, and renovation (PCI.7.5).

KEY CONCEPTS

- Manage Infection Risks in Utility Systems
- Establish a Safe Environment
- Assess Infection Risk During Demolition, Renovation, and Construction

KEY CONCEPT

Manage Infection Risks in Utility Systems

Preventing Waterborne Infectious Agents

Health care organizations must develop strategies for preventing and controlling waterborne infections. To do that effectively, you will first need to be familiar with water systems in health care facilities, the types of waterborne infectious diseases, and how they are transmitted.

Pathogens reside and multiply in reservoirs. A common pathogen that can cause significant harm to certain patients is *Legionella*. *Pseudomonas aeruginosa* is another organism that flourishes in water and poses infection risk to patients. If a component of a water distribution system in your facility is contaminated, it could become a breeding ground for these

Chapter 7 | Manage Infection Prevention and Control in the Environment of Care

pathogens. Components of a water distribution system typically include the following:

- **Cooling towers:** Water containment systems used to cool water for air-conditioning in an HVAC refrigeration system, or other system.
- **Hot and cold water systems:** Hot and cold water systems are used for washing, cooking, cleaning, clinical services, and other specialized functions. Most water distribution systems in health care facilities are hot and cold. Hot water systems provide the most likely growth areas for pathogens.
- **Aerosolizing water systems:** These systems are routed for water distribution that can be sprayed or aerosolized (including humidifiers, evaporative coolers, and decorative water features).

Strategies for preventing and controlling transmission of waterborne agents: Preventing waterborne infectious agents requires a game plan. Strategies include the following:

- Make contingency plans for provision of potable water during periods of contamination or disruption.
- Institute a program for maintaining and monitoring dialysis system water and dialysate quality.
- Follow the Association for the Advancement of Medical Instrumentation (AAMI) guidelines. You can find the guidelines at http://my.aami.org/store/detail.aspx?id=13959.
- Take inventory of all water inlets connected to main water lines, such as water fountains, ice machines, dental units, and automated endoscope reprocessors.
- Perform an annual risk assessment for *Legionella* (*see* page 137) in cooling towers and potable water.
- Implement a surveillance program to detect health care–associated infections (HAIs) resulting from *Legionella*.
- Institute a program for inhibiting the growth of *Legionella* in the potable water system and in cooling towers.

135

> ### Infection Control Regulations for Utility Systems
>
> To mitigate the risk of infection from utilities, The Joint Commission recommends that your organization involve credentialed professionals who adhere to the rules and regulations of organizations such as the American Society of Heating, Refrigerating and Air-Conditioning Engineers (ASHRAE) and the Facility Guidelines Institute (FGI) regarding the maintenance, design, and construction of water systems. These organizations have guidelines that can help you manage infection risks in utility systems, including the following:
> - *FGI Guidelines for Design and Construction of Health Care Facilities* (known as the FGI Guidelines): http://www.madcad.com/store/subscription/FGI-Guidelines-HOP-2010/
> - ASHRAE's *HVAC Design Manual for Hospitals and Clinics*: https://www.ashrae.org/technical-resources/bookstore/hvac-design-manual-for-hospitals-and-clinics
> - *ASHRAE Handbook: HVAC Applications*: https://www.ashrae.org/technical-resources/ashrae-handbook/description-2015-ashrae-handbook-hvac-applications

Legionella: *Legionella* is a bacterium that thrives and colonizes in stagnant water. Its transmission requires heat, stasis, and aerosolization, which are common factors in cooling towers, hot and cold water supply systems, faucets and showers, humidifiers, water heaters, and fountains. *Legionella*'s prevalence in water systems makes it a necessary target in your IC plan.

Without careful attention, *Legionella* can contaminate potable water and proliferate in your facility's water supply. This can lead to outbreaks of Legionnaires' disease, a serious, pneumonia-like illness caused by the bacteria. Immunocompromised patients (such as cancer patients) are the most susceptible to this organism, and deaths have occurred.

- **Preventing *Legionella*:** The best ways to monitor and control the growth of *Legionella* and other bacteria is to perform inspections and periodic maintenance of your water-based utilities, according to the US Occupational Safety and Health

Chapter 7 | Manage Infection Prevention and Control in the Environment of Care

One Health Care Facility's Legionnaires' Disease Story

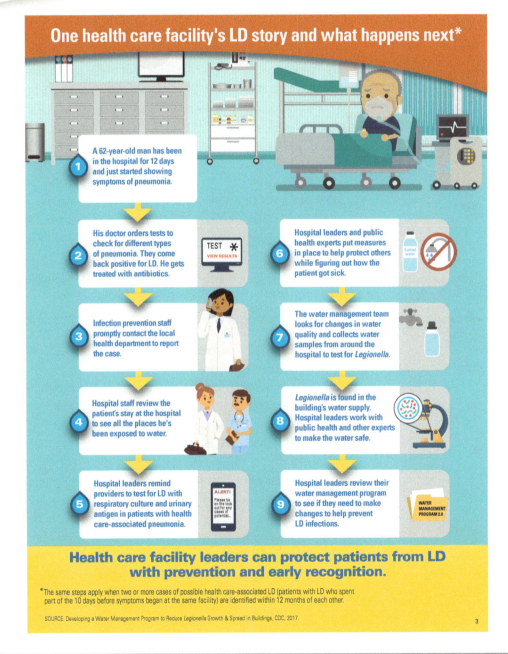

smart questions:

Are clinical staff aware of infection risks associated with water systems? Do they know when they should report issues to infection preventionists or facilities directors?

Administration (OSHA). Different methods of inspection and maintenance are required for each component of your facility's water distribution system. In the United States, OSHSA suggests the following for each system:
- Cooling towers: Locate cooling towers so that their drift is directed away from air intakes. OSHA suggests a twice-yearly cleaning that includes drift eliminators, which removes water droplets from the exhaust air. Algicides and biocides should be used during regular maintenance.
- Hot and cold water systems: For these systems, and aerosolizing water systems, you will need to maintain proper water temperature to minimize bacterial growth. Cold water systems should be kept at or below 68°F (20°C). Hot water systems should be kept at 140°F (60°C) or higher. Monitor the system water temperatures regularly.

OSHA also offers some additional system maintenance guidelines in Chapter 7 of its technical manual, found here: https://www.osha.gov/dts/osta/otm/otm_iii/otm_iii_7.html. OSHA recommends you do the following:
- Maintain sump temperatures at 68°F (20°C) to limit the growth of *legionella* and similar organisms.
- Inspect systems monthly and drain and clean quarterly.
- Clean and disinfect new systems. Their exposure to construction material residue can promote *Legionella* growth.
- Clean and disinfect out-of-service systems before returning to service.
- Treat circulating water with biocides and rust inhibitors continuously.

Legionella is not the only pathogen that can be spread through the water supply. Mold infection from fungi such as *Aspergillus* and *Fusarium*, and some types of bacteria, including *Pseudomonas*, have also been linked to water-based infection outbreaks.

Preventing Infection Risks Associated with HVAC Systems

When it comes to infection risks and utilities, it's vital to look at your HVAC systems. As we discussed earlier, bacteria forms in

Chapter 7 | **Manage Infection Prevention and Control in the Environment of Care**

reservoirs. HVAC systems can serve as reservoirs, as well as sources of infections.

To prevent infection risks associated with HVAC systems, your IC team should become familiar with airborne infectious diseases that can be transmitted, the basic components and operations of HVAC systems, and pressure relationships, air-exchange rates, and filtration. Start by reviewing publications about HVAC systems and infectious diseases associated with these systems, such as the following:

- **Guidelines for Environmental Infection Control in Health-Care Facilities:** This guide by the US Centers for Disease Control and Prevention (CDC) offers recommendations from the CDC's Healthcare Infection Control Practices Advisory Committee (HICPAC), including handling air systems and mitigating airborne contaminants: https://www.cdc.gov /infectioncontrol/pdf/guidelines/environmental-guidelines.pdf.
- **HVAC Design Manual for Hospitals and Clinics:** This guide by American Society of Heating, Refrigerating and Air-Conditioning Engineers (ASHRAE) provides those involved in the design, installation, and commissioning of HVAC systems for hospitals and clinics with a comprehensive reference source for their work. It covers IC and gives best-practice recommendations on temperature, humidity, air exchange, and pressure requirements for various types of rooms found in hospitals: https://www.ashrae.org/technical-resources /bookstore/hvac-design-manual-for-hospitals-and-clinics.
- **Guidelines for Design and Construction of Hospitals / Guidelines for Design and Construction of Outpatient Facilities:** These guides by the Facility Guidelines Institute (FGI) are useful resources when learning about HVAC systems and associated risks. They address indoor air-quality standards, including ventilation rates, temperatures, humidity levels, pressure relationships, and minimum air changes per hour specific to different areas of health care facilities: https:// www.fgiguidelines.org/guidelines/2018-fgi-guidelines/.

Infection control in HVAC systems: An HVAC system can help prevent the spread of infectious agents or it can proliferate them, depending on the design, installation, and maintenance of the system and three variables that factor into its operation: air pressurization, air change rates, and filtration.

139

Pressure relationships: *Room pressurization* refers to the direction air is forced into or out of a room by the HVAC system when all doors are closed. The offset in airflow from surrounding areas to a room, or vice versa, is the pressure relationship. Positive pressure forces air out of the room and is essential in areas such as operating rooms or special procedure rooms. Negative pressure draws air in from surrounding areas and is important for patients who have contracted infectious diseases such as tuberculosis. Keep contaminants from moving into critical areas by controlling pressure via an offset between supply-air and exhaust-air volumes.

The ability to control pressure relationships in rooms is extremely important in special-care units that treat patients who are highly susceptible to infection, such as organ transplant recipients and chemotherapy patients. These areas include the following:

- Operating rooms
- Special procedure rooms
- Delivery rooms
- Airborne infection isolation rooms (AIIRs)
- Laboratories
- Sterile supply rooms
- Biohazardous waste storage areas
- Protective environments—positive-pressure rooms for immunosuppressed patients designed to minimize fungal spore counts in the air and reduce fungal infections

Air pressurization must be monitored in rooms. This requires routine maintenance to check monitoring devices and sensor calibration.

Air change rates: The rate at which outdoor air replaces indoor air within a room is the air change rate. The number of times per hour that the HVAC system replaces the entire volume of air contained within a room is referred to as air changes (ACH). The higher the ACH, the faster potential contaminants will be removed from the room.

During unoccupied periods, regulations typically allow a reduction in minimum total airflow rates to save your organization

Chapter 7 | Manage Infection Prevention and Control in the Environment of Care

energy. This is achieved by using a variable air volume (VAV) tracking system, which regulates the airflow in a room to meet rising or falling temperatures. FGI Guidelines and ASHRAE allow ventilation rates to be reduced to 25% of the occupied period rates, as long as continuous directional control and room pressurization are maintained, and full ventilation ACH rates can be reestablished when a room is occupied.

Factors in determining the effectiveness of a VAV HVAC system:

- Hours of operation of spaces being served by the HVAC system
- Magnitude of the difference between the required minimum ventilation ACH and the airflow required to maintain appropriate temperature as measured by thermometer freely exposed to the air
- Requirements for controlling the direction of airflow

Filtration: Filtration removes potentially harmful particulates from circulating air. Effective HVAC systems may include multiple high-efficiency particulate air (HEPA) filters filtration units to help minimize particles in high-risk areas, such as intensive care areas, laboratories, and the operating room. Filtration is the main defense against fungi in ventilation systems. HEPA filters and most prefilters are effective against fungi, if installed correctly and well maintained. Fungi can grow in filters as well, so the CDC recommends metal-framed filters over wooden ones. Your filters must be changed regularly, according to manufacturer guidelines.

Complying with Joint Commission requirements for HVAC:

To comply with the Joint Commission requirements for HVAC systems, you must do the following:

- Develop and implement evidence-based policies and procedures for ensuring the proper maintenance and functioning of HVAC systems in the facility.
- Document routine monitoring of air-handling systems in special-care areas—airborne infection isolation areas, operating rooms, and so forth. Malfunctions should also be documented.
- Implement strategies for IC during demolition, construction, and renovation (*see* page 147).

in other words
HEPA filters

HEPA is an acronym for "high-efficiency particulate air" or "high-efficiency particulate arrestance." A HEPA filter works by forcing air through a fine mesh that traps harmful particles. To qualify as HEPA by industry standards, an air filter must remove 99.97% of particles with a diameter of 0.3 microns. Current CDC *Guidelines for Environmental Infection Control in Health-Care Facilities* recommend HEPA filtration for the capture of pathogens, microbial spores, and other contaminants in the air.

JCI Standard PCI.8.1 describes how HEPA filtration systems can be used as a short-term measure for creating temporary negative-pressure isolation (TNPI) in lieu of negative pressure for isolation rooms in particular circumstances. Use of TNPI must follow acceptable guidelines and adhere to building and fire codes.

Infection control and HVAC system maintenance: Regular maintenance on HVAC system components such as fans, coils, belts, and filters is needed for them to function properly. Your team will need to establish preventive maintenance, cleaning, and inspection schedules for the HVAC system. The schedules should also be written into the IC plan. Remember to always keep up-to-date records of maintenance activities and requested maintenance.

HVAC systems maintenance tasks: The following are some common maintenance tasks for components of HVAC systems in health care organizations:
- Change filters when a manometer reading indicates that they are dirty in accordance with the manufacturer's performance measures.
- Adjust louvers and dampers for air balance.
- Keep automatic controls in good working order.
- Thoroughly clean ducts if they become contaminated.
- Change pulleys and belts as needed.
- Clean screens and keep them tight.
- Periodically calibrate and test negative-pressure alarms.

KEY CONCEPT

Establish a Safe Environment

Contaminated surfaces contribute to the transmission of pathogens, which can survive and remain virulent for long periods of time.

To ensure that environmental surfaces are safe and comply with Joint Commission Standard EC.02.06.01, your organization must devise clearly defined cleaning and disinfection policies and procedures, use evidence-based monitoring, and ensure compliance with environmental services and housekeeping protocols

Daily Patient Room Cleaning Procedure Checklist
This tool can be used to ensure that all necessary cleaning of patients' rooms are performed daily. It can also serve as a record of that cleaning.

142

Chapter 7 | Manage Infection Prevention and Control in the Environment of Care

for surfaces. These surfaces commonly include floors, walls, furnishings, sinks, carpets, and curtains.

For international organizations, the relevant standard is PCI.9, which requires that staff be educated in proper hand-washing, hand-disinfection, and surface-disinfection procedures, as well as proper use of personal protective equipment. Measureable Element (ME) 3 of that standard requires the organization to implement surface disinfecting procedures for areas and situations in the facility that could lead to infection.

Environmental Cleaning and Disinfection

Your organization must determine which cleaners and disinfectants to use and how they should be used. The selection should be based on evidence-based information. In addition, your IC team will need to develop policies and protocols that include the following:

- Selecting cleaners and disinfectants, and trialing and evaluating them
- Using cleaners and disinfectants properly
- Training staff and testing competency for using cleaners and disinfectants
- Monitoring cleaning and disinfection practices, and evaluating them
- Ensuring a standardization of products across departments
- Approving new products through a multidisciplinary organizational committee
- Using appropriate tools and products for cleaning and disinfecting

Many types of cleaners and disinfectants are available, and they are continuously evolving. Although liquid disinfectants are common, newer technologies, such as ultraviolet light systems and vaporized hydrogen peroxide, have been shown to be more effective at reducing the amount of bacteria living on a surface.

Strategies for evaluating environmental cleaning:

The Joint Commission requires that interior spaces meet the needs of the patient population and are safe and suitable to the care, treatment, and services provided. This includes cleanliness.

in other words

Bioburden

Bioburden is the number of bacteria living on a surface that has not been sterilized. The term is most often used in the context of bioburden testing, also known as microbial limit testing, which is performed on pharmaceutical products and medical products for quality control purposes. For example, when endoscopes are not cleaned adequately, there may be significant bioburden of organisms left on the device that can be transmitted to the next patient.

143

Thorough cleaning with detergent and water removes most microorganisms and other contaminants and is usually adequate for surfaces and items remote from the patient.

All surfaces and equipment that have been in contact with blood or other potentially infectious materials require disinfection. These items must be cleaned first with a soap-and-water solution and then treated with an antimicrobial product—such as bleach or a chemical disinfectant—because the presence of blood and proteins interferes with some antimicrobial products.

The CDC has produced options for evaluating environmental cleaning of environmental surfaces. The agency's strategies include the following:
- Develop and implement policies and procedures for cleaning and disinfecting environmental surfaces and handling laundry and medical waste.
- Conduct a risk assessment to identify appropriate care for high-touch surfaces.
- Define high-touch areas by department (each area will be different).
- Assign responsibility for cleaning and disinfecting areas, environmental surfaces, and objects.
- Ensure that cleaning and disinfecting agents and equipment are appropriately used and do not damage surfaces.
- Ensure that procedures for cleaning and disinfection comply with evidence-based recommendations, regulations, and requirements.
- Provide continuous training on cleaning and disinfection processes, including hand hygiene, changing gloves, and safe handling of linen and trash.
- Institute monitoring of environmental services personnel to ensure that they use appropriate practices and types of cleaners and disinfectants.
- Take a multidisciplinary team approach for evaluating environment of care issues. Members of a multidisciplinary team could include personnel from IC, environmental services, facilities maintenance, safety, performance improvement, and nursing services. An environmental rounds tool is a useful guide. Here's one from the Association for

Chapter 7 | Manage Infection Prevention and Control in the Environment of Care

Professionals in Infection Control and Epidemiology (APIC): https://apic.org/Resource_/TinyMceFileManager/Academy /ASC_101_resources/Assessment_Checklist/Environment _Checklist.doc.

- Share audit findings with environmental services personnel.
- Reinforce the importance of preventing infection on a continual basis.
- Assess the cleaning and disinfection competence of environmental services and housekeeping personnel.
- Recognize staff for their efforts and reward accomplishments.

COLLABORATION: Collaboration between IC and environmental services personnel is essential for success in providing a clean, safe, and functional environment and decreasing rates of HAIs.

Monitor the Effectiveness of Cleaning and Disinfection Methods

Your organization should implement a program to monitor cleaning and disinfection practices. Your IC team will need to determine which methods are appropriate at your facility. The CDC offers some examples of monitoring you might use:

- **Direct observation:** A covert, visual assessment of cleaning practices can be used to ensure that staff are following cleaning policies and procedures. However, logistical issues related to maintaining such a program outside a research setting may limit adoption of this form of monitoring. The complexity of covertly monitoring cleaning practice in individual patient rooms without the evaluator being recognized may also be an issue. In addition, an eye test is not a reliable indicator of whether surfaces are actually being decontaminated. To find out if infectious microbes are being eliminated regularly, you'll need additional methods of testing.
- **Swab cultures:** Swab cultures are easy to use, but they are costly and the results are generally poor indicators for assessing disinfection practices. Other issues that may limit the broad application of this system include the delay in analyzing results, the need to determine precleaning levels of contamination for each object evaluated to accurately

assess cleaning practice, and the limited feasibility of monitoring multiple surfaces in multiple patient rooms as part of an ongoing monitoring program. If this method is used, the microbiology laboratory must agree to grow the cultures from the swabs.

- **Agar slide plates:** Agar coated glass slides with finger holds were developed to simplify quantitative cultures of liquids. These slides have been adopted for use in environmental surface monitoring. Although there may be some difficulties using agar slide cultures on surfaces that aren't large and flat, they potentially provide an easy method for quantifying viable microbial surface contamination for some surfaces. Similar to swab cultures, there is a need to determine precleaning levels of contamination for each object evaluated in order to accurately assess cleaning practice.

- **Fluorescent markers:** Fluorescent gel, powder, and lotion have all been developed for marking high-touch objects prior to room cleaning. Fluorescent markers are easily applied and can be a very useful tool to educate personnel and evaluate cleaning processes. Fluorescent gel dries transparent on surfaces, resists abrasion, and can help objectively evaluate cleaning practice. Powder and lotion may have limited use in a monitoring system because they can be disturbed easily and aren't easy to remove.

- **Adenosine triphosphate (ATP) bioluminescence:** ATP measures only organic debris but can be used for assessing how well things are cleaned. A specialized swab is used to sample a standardized surface area, which is then analyzed using a portable handheld luminometer. The total amount of ATP, both microbial and nonmicrobial, is quantified and expressed as relative light units. Very high readings may represent either a viable bioburden, organic debris including dead bacteria, or a combination of both. The ATP system has been used to document significant improvement in daily cleaning and provide quantitative measurement of cleanliness on high-touch surfaces.

No matter what monitoring approach you choose, the CDC says it must be performed by epidemiologists, infection preventionists, or their qualified designees who are not part of

Chapter 7 | Manage Infection Prevention and Control in the Environment of Care

the cleaning program. This assures the validity of the information collected. You can find additional information on monitoring cleaning and disinfection practices on the CDC website at https://www.cdc.gov/hai/toolkits/appendices-evaluating-environ-cleaning.html.

KEY CONCEPT

Assess Infection Risk During Demolition, Renovation, and Construction

Joint Commission Standard EC.02.06.05 and its elements of performance (EPs) require your organization to manage its environment during demolition, renovation, or new construction to reduce risk to those in the organization. Whereas JCI Standard PCI.7.5 requires international organizations to reduce the risk of infection associated with mechanical and engineering controls and during demolition, construction, and renovation. A risk assessment prior to work on such projects is also required for international organizations.

Design criteria: When planning for new, altered, or renovated space, your facility may use one of the following design criteria:

- State rules and regulations.
- *Guidelines for Design and Construction of Health Care Facilities*, 2014 edition, administered by the Facility Guidelines Institute and published by the American Society for Health Care Engineering (ASHE).
- Other reputable standards and guidelines provide equivalent design criteria should the above rules, regulations, and guidelines not meet specific design needs.

Risk assessment: When planning for demolition, construction, or renovation, the organization must conduct a preconstruction risk assessment for air quality requirements, IC, utility require-ments, noise, vibration, and other hazards that affect care, treatment, and services.

Mimimize risk: Take action based on your assessment to minimize risks during demolition, construction, or renovation.

147

Strategies for compliance: To comply with requirements, your team will need to take steps to implement IC measures for internal construction and repair projects. Here are some recommendations from the CDC:

Prepare for the project
- Establish a multidisciplinary team that includes IC staff to coordinate demolition, construction, and renovation projects. The team should identify preventive measures that mitigate the effects of demolition, construction, and renovation activities on air quality, water, and HVAC systems, environmental cleanliness, and traffic flow.
- Document the multidisciplinary team's activities in design, demolition, construction, and renovation activities.
- Complete a preconstruction risk assessment, including an infection control risk assessment (ICRA). (*See* the construction risk assessment matrix in "Tools of the Trade.") A preconstruction risk assessment includes the following:
  - Disruption of essential services
  - Relocation or placement of patients
  - Barrier placements to control airborne contaminants
  - Debris cleanup and removal
  - Traffic flow
- Secure an IC permit for demolition, construction, and renovation activities. This tool can be used to document and communicate with contractors about their responsibilities during the preconstruction risk assessment. It can also be used to document follow-up visits by the infection preventionist or safety manager. You can find a sample of an IC permit at the ASHE website: http://www.ashe.org/resources/tools/pdfs/assessment_icra.pdf.

Educate staff
- Institute a multidisciplinary program for training, monitoring, and promoting adherence to IC regulations and practices during construction, demolition, and renovation.
- Provide educational materials in languages for all workers.
- Require construction workers and subcontractors to participate in IC training.

in other words

Infection control risk assessment

An infection control risk assessment, or ICRA, is a multidisciplinary, organizational, documented process that carefully considers your facility's patient population and program and then does the following:
- Focuses on reduction of risk from infection
- Acts through phases of facility planning, design, construction, renovation, and facility maintenance
- Coordinates and weighs knowledge about infection, infectious agents, and the care environment, permitting the organization to anticipate potential impact.

Chapter 7 | Manage Infection Prevention and Control in the Environment of Care

Post warning notices
- Post signs clearly identifying construction or demolition areas and potential hazards.
- Mark detours for pedestrians to avoid any work areas.

Separate patients from construction activities
- Identify patient populations for relocation based on the ICRA.
- Arrange for patient transfers before construction begins to avoid delays.
- Provide at-risk patients with protective respiratory equipment if necessary.
- Transport patients on different elevators than those used for construction materials.
- Establish alternative traffic patterns for staff, patients, and visitors, away from the risk assessment, construction, or demolition activities.
- Designate through-areas, such as hallways and elevators, for construction worker use only.

Monitor Infection Control Activities for Internal Construction and Repair Projects

After a construction, demolition, or renovation project begins, you'll want to monitor activities as they go to ensure that IC procedures are being followed. Joint Commission Standard EC.04.01.01 requires your organization to collect information to monitor conditions in the environment. Similarly, JCI Standard PCI.7.5 requires organizations to assess and manage risks and the impact of demolition, renovation, or construction on air quality and IC activities. To do this you should set up a monitoring program, based on environmental tours or rounds.

Environmental tours: These rounds are valuable tools for assessing risks and evaluating how your IC practices are applied at your facility. Conducted at least every six months in patient care areas and at least annually in nonpatient care areas, the tours should be performed by a multidisciplinary team that includes personnel from IC, supervisory and nonsupervisory staff from the area being surveyed, safety, housekeeping, facilities maintenance, and other areas.

Environmental Rounds Worksheet for Infection Prevention
Use this worksheet to perform environmental tours for infection control in your organization.

149

Each tour should be held on a set schedule and be documented using a standardized form for consistency throughout departments. The tours should also be used to create a process for reporting findings, along with corrective measures and performance improvement recommendations. The reports should be sent to members of the multidisciplinary team and to your organization leaders who can greenlight improvements. The tours can be used as evidence for performance improvement activities your organization develops and implements.

The CDC recommends that, in addition to conducting environmental tours, organizations create a daily process for monitoring and documenting the airflow in isolation rooms and the positive airflow in protective environment rooms. This is particularly important when patients requiring isolation precautions are in these rooms.

TOOLS OF THE TRADE

- Daily Patient Room Cleaning Procedure Checklist
- Environmental Rounds Worksheet for Infection Prevention

Additional Resources

You can find out more about *Legionella*, including disease specifics, clinical features, and diagnosis, treatment, and prevention at http://www.cdc.gov/legionella/clinicians.html.

For more recommendations for environmental cleaning and disinfection practices, download the Options for Evaluating Environmental Cleaning and other related material here: https://www.cdc.gov/hai/toolkits/evaluating-environmental-cleaning.html

CHAPTER 8

Evaluate and Improve Your Infection Prevention and Control Plan

You've put together your infection prevention and control (IC) plan and implemented it, but is it effective? That's where performance evaluation comes in. Evaluation of an IC program is essential to determine if the surveillance, prevention initiatives, and improvement strategies are effectively reducing risk and infections. Without an intentional evaluation process, the IC team and leaders will not know if the program is delivering value to patient safety. The Joint Commission addresses the concept of evaluation in Infection Prevention and Control (IC) Standard IC.03.01.01. For organizations accredited by Joint Commission International (JCI), the related requirement is Prevention and Control of Infections (PCI) Standard PCI.10, Measurable Element (ME) 3: Monitoring data are used to evaluate and support improvements to the IC program.

KEY CONCEPTS

- Evaluate Your Performance
- Drive Improvement

KEY CONCEPT

Evaluate Your Performance

Evaluating Infection Prevention and Control Plan Performance

Your IC evaluation process should include a careful review of all the components of your plan. This should be done by your IC Committee or the multidisciplinary team that developed and maintains your IC plan. Reviewing these components will help drive improvement and will guide your planning for the following year. Consider the following steps:

- Identifying and prioritizing risks
- Developing and revising goals
- Implementing and evaluating interventions
- Sharing evaluation results organizationally
- Making plan revisions

Components of an effective evaluation report: An effective evaluation helps determine if your IC program is addressing the most prevalent risks (as identified in your risk assessment and surveillance activities) and meeting its goals and objectives. The following components should be considered in your evaluation process:

- Progress toward achieving goals and objectives (process and outcome measures)
- Program objectives, and whether or not they should be revised or removed; or whether new objectives should be added
- Program successes and failures from the previous year

Your evaluation, based on these three components, should be used in the next risk assessment and program revision process. When making an evaluation, the process should be multi-disciplinary and collaborative. It should take into account all programs and services within your organization and evaluate risks specific to your organization.

An evaluation report should include, at minimum, the following components:

Chapter 8 | Evaluate and Improve Your Infection Prevention and Control Plan

- **Organizational and internal or external changes:** Describe the changes that influenced the scope of the infection surveillance, prevention, and control program/plan. Include any significant events that altered the scope and goals of your IC program, such as emerging infectious diseases. For example, during 2014–2016 some health care organizations needed to act quickly to handle patients infected with Ebola, as well as protect other patients, visitors, and staff from infection.
- **IC program objective/goal review:** Include any activities that met the program goals, and any data that show how measurable objectives are being achieved. Evaluation may include the following:
  - Quantitative data such as rate graphs and tables (for example, infection rates and compliance rates for process measures)
  - Qualitative data such as patient feedback
  - Observation results used to measure hand hygiene, environmental cleaning, or isolation precautions practices
- **Summary of important, non-goal issues:** Describe activity that was not part of a specific objective. Examples may include new construction activities, or an emergency situation that occurred. These activities may become objectives for next year.
- **Summary of special-cause investigations:** Special-cause investigations performed during the year may include cluster or outbreak investigations.
- **Description of challenges:** Any barriers or difficulties that your team experienced over the year should be documented, as well as any actions implemented to overcome them. For example, your organization may have experienced a drop in hand hygiene compliance rates or an uptick in the number of health care–associated infections (HAIs) associated with endoscopes.

Identifying and prioritizing risks: The evaluation process should assess infection risks that are specific to your organization, both internally and externally. For example, if surgical procedures occur in your facility, assess for surgical site

infections. If there was a meningitis outbreak in your surrounding community since your last risk assessment, examine how prepared your organization is to address that illness.

A risk assessment will help identify and prioritize risks and allow you to focus on any changes that need to be made to the IC program. Typically, you will begin by analyzing known and common risks, but you'll also need to assess potential events, such as an influenza pandemic or other significant outbreak, and how it might affect your facility. Review current scientific literature and reports from agencies such as the US Centers for Disease Control and Prevention (CDC) and state departments of health or national or regional ministries of health to help prepare for possible risk scenarios (*see* Chapter 3 for strategies for assessing risk).

- **How to prioritize risks:** Time and resources are required to identify every risk. You may not have a lot of both, so make sure to start by focusing on issues that have the potential to do the most serious harm. Your IC team, risk assessment team, and safety/quality committee should work together to determine which risks should be priorities for your IC program. The decision should be based on their data, information, and experience. Remember that your leaders will need to approve any plans for prioritized risks. After they are approved, your prioritized risks will help to shape the development of your IC goals and objectives.

For more on risk assessment strategies, *see* Chapter 3.

Developing and revising goals: The purpose of Joint Commission Standard IC.03.01.01 and its elements of performance (EPs), and JCI Standard PCI.10, ME 3, is to guide your organization in carefully reviewing its IC program so you can determine if your goals were achieved, or how your plan can be improved. Goals are developed based on the most significant risks to the patients, staff, and visitors to your facility.

Ultimately, the IC goals you establish should be aligned with your organization's overall goals. If your organization's goals or strategies change, you may need to adjust the IC goals to keep them in line. Many goals will carry over from year to year, but

smart questions:

How do you communicate your organization's IC goals to staff?

Chapter 8 | Evaluate and Improve Your Infection Prevention and Control Plan

reassessing them annually is important to properly plan and prioritize risks to patients and staff, based on potential threats and environmental factors. For example, if your organization establishes a goal for reducing overall patient safety events by 20% during a 12-month period, identify which events during the previous year involved HAIs. You may find that 5% of the previous year's patient safety events involved health care–associated urinary tract infections, for instance. In that case, implement steps to reduce those infections.

The evaluation process will allow you to determine which activities in your IC program had the biggest impact on improving patient safety in the past year. Those activities and the goals they fall under should be repeated. Because they've already proven helpful, it may be possible to expand on their success. If a performance improvement project designed to ensure that nonessential cardiac catheters are removed as soon as possible led to a reduction in central line–associated bloodstream infections (CLABSIs), then continue that project to achieve further CLABSI reductions, or apply those methods to another IC process, such as removal of nonessential urinary catheters.

The evaluation will also reveal which goals must be revised or replaced, due to performance that did not meet expectations. For example, if your personal protective equipment (PPE) program for handling infectious materials has not resulted in improved practices, consider bolstering your efforts by doing the following:

- Identifying the disconnect between your established regulations and practices, and the actual staff practices at your facility
- Determining changes that can bridge that divide, such as increasing accessibility of alcohol-based hand rub dispensers to improve hand hygiene, or identifying areas in which staff need additional training—such as which environmental surfaces require cleaning versus disinfection
- Offering additional education and training to increase staff compliance with proper PPE use
- Implementing a system that assesses PPE compliance through staff surveys or direct observation of staff practices during rounds

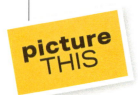

Infection Prevention and Control Program
Annual Evaluation Process

This figure illustrates the ongoing evaluation process as part of the infection prevention and control (IPC) program.

Chapter 8 | **Evaluate and Improve Your Infection Prevention and Control Plan**

Sharing evaluation results: Whenever you do a risk assessment, it's vital to let your leaders and other stakeholders in your organization know about the findings. Communicating any problems or issues that have been flagged during the year, as well as IC program successes is also important. Findings from the evaluation must be communicated at least annually to the individuals or interdisciplinary group that manages the patient safety program.

When you do communicate the evaluation results, consider the following questions:

- Where do you find the information needed for the report? You'll gather information from your IC activities such as surveillance and monitoring activities performed by various departments.
- What information should be included in the report? A summary report that features data on HAIs and goals for the next year is fine. Or you can include a review of all IC activities, investigations, and findings.
- Who should receive the evaluation results? You'll want to inform anyone who can use the information to improve patient care. That includes leadership, medical staff leaders or medical directors, IC Committee members, and other key staff.
- How should the information be reported? To be effective, the information should be available in a written report and presented verbally to those in your organization who can assist with and champion IC activities and goals.

Try creating a reporting template to organize your risk assessment findings, as well as the results from addressing priority risks. Following are some examples of the information your template could include:

- Highest-priority and continuing risks
- Goals and objectives for each risk
- Strategies developed to achieve risk reduction
- Individuals and departments responsible
- Progress toward achieving the objective or target
- Objective or goal met
- Objective or goal not met
- Actions or recommendations for IC program revision

157

A gap analysis is one way of accomplishing this. A gap analysis is a tool that compares your organization's actual performance against its potential or desired performance. *See* the example in Table 8-1 below.

Table 8-1. Sample Gap Analysis for Infection Prevention and Control Risk Assessment

Area/Issue/Topic/Standard	Current Status	Desired Status	Gap (Describe)	Action Plan and Evaluation	Priority: High, Medium, Low
Incomplete implementation of CDC Hand Hygiene (HH) Guideline (NPSG.07.01.01)	• Guideline is approved by ICC. • Required elements are not implemented throughout the organization.	Ensure full implementation of required elements throughout the organization by December 2017, e.g., Category IA, IB, IC.	Only 60% of units and services are following CDC HH guideline and organization policy.	• Develop proactive implementation plan. • Make a leadership priority. • Obtain all necessary supplies. • Evaluate existing HH compliance. • Provide feedback to staff monthly. • Ensure full implementation by December 2017 for all units and services.	High
Systematic and proactive surveillance activity to determine usual endemic rates of infections (IC.01.03.01, EP 3)	• Current surveillance is periodic. • There is retrospective chart review of a few selected infections. • Data are not always analyzed in a timely manner.	Attain prospective surveillance for selected infections and populations on an ongoing basis using NHSN methodology; obtained by June 2017.	• There is a lack of IPC staff and computer support to perform concurrent and ongoing surveillance. • There is an absence of a well-designed surveillance plan. • Access to laboratory data is difficult.	• Request funding to join NHSN and obtain computer and software to enter and analyze data. • Teach IPC staff about surveillance methodologies and how to use NHSN methodology. • Work with laboratory director or contracted service to design access system for microbiology and other reports. • Assess program status in 6 months.	Medium to High
Inconsistent cleaning of high-touch areas in patient care settings (IC.02.01.01)	Data from environmental services supervisor and nursing observations indicate that high-touch surfaces are being cleaned with appropriate frequency per hospital policy only 58% of the time.	• Environmental services or nursing staff per policy clean high-touch surfaces at least daily and when visibly soiled with the hospital approved disinfectant using correct technique. • Attain at least 95% compliance by June 2017.	• Time for daily cleaning of patient rooms may not be adequate based on current EVS staffing ratios. • There is a lack of emphasis on potential outcomes from pathogen transmission from contaminated high-touch areas.	• Request review of staffing of EVS personnel for areas requiring frequent high-touch cleaning. • Emphasize policy and necessity for nursing staff to clean high-touch areas in patient care settings on a regular basis and when visibly soiled. • Work with EVS and nursing leaders to accomplish goals. • Continue to monitor and provide feedback to staff.	Medium to High

continued

Chapter 8 | Evaluate and Improve Your Infection Prevention and Control Plan

Table 8-1. Sample Gap Analysis for Infection Prevention and Control Risk Assessment
continued

Area/Issue/Topic/ Standard	Current Status	Desired Status	Gap (Describe)	Action Plan and Evaluation	Priority: High, Medium, Low
Needlestick injuries in employees increasing (IC.02.03.01)	The incidence of needlesticks among EVS staff is 3%. Analysis shows that greatest risk is during changing of needle containers.	• Reduce needlesticks in EVS staff to equal to or less than 0.2% during next 6 months by January 2018. • Maintain low rate thereafter among all EVS staff.	• Observations show that needle containers are often overflowing. • There is confusion among nursing and housekeeping staff about responsibility and timing for emptying or changing containers. • Nursing supervisors are not aware of issue.	• Clarify policy and repeat education to staff about criteria for filling/changing needle containers. • Discuss situation with nurse managers and EVS staff—emphasize responsibility. • Display ongoing data to show number of weeks without needlesticks. • Reevaluate needlestick injuries in 3 and 6 months and report to staff and ICC. • Evaluate processes implemented for improvement.	Medium to High

To complete the gap analysis, identify the issue and describe the current status, the desired status, and the gap between the two. State the action plan to "close" the gap and evaluation process. Indicate priority among risk issues for the organization. CDC, US Centers for Disease Control and Prevention; NPSG, National Patient Safety Goal: IC, Infection Prevention and Control; EP, element of performance; ICC, Infection Control Committee; NHSN, National Healthcare Safety Network; IPC, Infection Prevention and Control (program); EVS, environmental services.

When you do report evaluation findings, make sure that anyone who receives it will be able to understand and interpret the data. You can make this easier by including the following:
- Graphics to enhance the written presentation
- Documented sources, using references
- A consistency to your presentation method

COLLABORATION: Staff from throughout your facility should be involved in the evaluation process because IC practices are the responsibility of everyone in the organization. A multi-disciplinary collaboration throughout the process, from risk assessment to evaluation, will give you a broad overview of risks associated with infections, and allows you to effectively characterize and prioritize infection risks, identify measures for reducing those risks, and develop goals and objectives.

Using findings to revise your plan: When you evaluate your IC program, you will likely uncover issues that should be incorporated into your next risk assessment. You will also use the

evaluation findings when revising your plan. Make sure the evaluation states what issues should become an IC program objective for next year. You can incorporate the written evaluation into the program or create a separate document. As mentioned, you will want to distribute this to the leaders and staff who need the information.

Data Use in Infection Prevention and Control

Data collection and analysis will tell you if your goals have been met and will continue to be met based on performance. Gathering and presenting data accurately, by using appropriate tools and following best practices, will help your organization to increase its chances for controlling and preventing the threat of infection in your facility.

COLLABORATION: To properly gather and analyze data, you will need to assemble a work group. Identify those leaders, managers, and others who can influence health care practices or provide technical support for data collection, management, and analysis. Collaborate with the group members to develop the program, create a written plan for surveillance and other data gathering activities, implement the plan, and evaluate the program on a consistent basis.

Data collection: In many cases, collecting performance data is a matter of simple observation, often aided by the use of checklists. Two particular forms of observation for collecting data on IC in the physical environment are popular with many organizations—rounds and interviews, which mirror some of the data collection used in tracers. There are three types of data you'll want to obtain, review, and analyze for your IC program. The categories include following:

Organizational data
- **Access key reports in the organization needed for the risk assessment**. This includes services provided, populations served, characteristics, special environmental issues, microbiological reports, and antibiotic use data.
- **Review IC program surveillance data**. This includes multidrug-resistant organism (MDRO) rates and trends.

Chapter 8 | Evaluate and Improve Your Infection Prevention and Control Plan

- **Assess organizational data**. This includes medical records, lab records, admission and discharge numbers.
- **Review sentinel event reports**. This includes risk reports, mortality data, and so forth.
- **Review institutional costs**. This includes the costs of HAIs and resistant organisms.

Scientific and professional data

- **Review the literature for new trends in IC**. Good sources include *Journal of the American Medical Association*, The *New England Journal of Medicine*, *Clinical Infectious Diseases*, *Pediatrics*, *Infection Control & Hospital Epidemiology*, *Joint Commission Journal on Quality and Patient Safety*, and *American Journal of Infection Control*.
- **Review IC information on key websites**. Examples include the US Centers for Disease Control and Prevention (CDC), World Health Organization (WHO), Association for Professionals in Infection Control and Epidemiology (APIC), Society for Healthcare Epidemiology of America (SHEA), Infectious Diseases Society of America (IDSA), and The Joint Commission. Health care organizations in the United States can also check with state and local health departments. International organizations should consider information from their respective ministries of health.
- **Review statements, recommendations, and guidelines from professional organizations**. Some good sites include SHEA, APIC, IDSA, Association of periOperative Registered Nurses (AORN), Association for the Advancement of Medical Instrumentation (AAMI), Facility Guidelines Institute (FGI), American Society of Health-System Pharmacists (ASHP), Agency for Healthcare Research and Quality (AHRQ), National Quality Forum (NQF), World Health Organization, ministries of health, and patient safety organizations.

Community data

- **Connect with the local health department or ministry of health to identify trends that may affect infection risk**. Risks may include emerging and reemerging pathogens, and infectious diseases in the community that could affect infection risk to patents and staff in the organization.
- **Review information concerning special high-risk and nonimmunized community populations**.

161

> **TRY THIS TOOL**
>
> **Performance Improvement Matrix**
> Performance improvement activities use a variety of tools in the collection and evaluation of data. Some tools are used to collect and display data for analysis, whereas others are used to help generate ideas, determine the root cause of a problem, or understand a process. Organizations need to know which tool to use for each purpose. This tool lists some common performance improvement tools and their uses.

Data analysis: Organizations can use competency data as indicators of performance. System deficiencies that complicate staff efforts to adhere to the IC policies and procedures can derail even the best and most effective plans. The Joint Commission and JCI have acknowledged this by requiring that accredited organizations assess each person's abilities to perform, which includes knowledge, skill, and behavior.

Using data, your organization can figure out where to focus on bolstering performance through education. The collection and aggregation of this competency data and the subsequent analysis is vital to getting the appropriate resources from leadership. Likewise, any data on your successes related to mitigating infection transmission will also help to gain buy-in and support from leadership.

Collecting and analyzing data will certainly be a challenge for you, particularly if your organization is small. Thankfully, the CDC *Guidelines for Environmental Infection Control in Health-Care Facilities* offers lots of helpful information to IC and environmental professionals. The guidelines suggest that your organization evaluate and adapt its recommendations by using the following to measure performance:

- **Specimen contamination**: Evaluate possible environmental sources (water, laboratory solutions, or reagents) of specimen contamination.
- **Construction**: Document whether IC personnel are actively involved in all demolition, construction, and renovation. A risk assessment of the necessary types of construction barriers is required. Daily monitoring and documenting of the presence of negative airflow within the construction zone or renovation area should be performed.
- **Protective environments (PEs)—positive-pressure rooms for immunosuppressed patients**: Monitor and document the negative airflow in sensitive areas, particularly when patients are in these rooms. (*See* Chapter 7 for more information about airflow.) This should be done daily.
- **Water quality testing**: Perform assays at least once a month by using standard quantitative methods to check water for bacteria.

Chapter 8 | Evaluate and Improve Your Infection Prevention and Control Plan

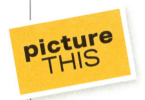

Effectiveness of Training in Decontamination Procedures

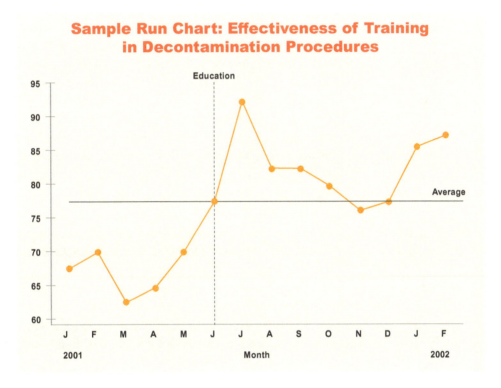

- **Water damage response**: Document policies to identify and respond to water damage. Wet materials should be repaired and dried or removed within 72 hours.

Reporting System for Staff

The staff in your organization have a responsibility to communicate about infections, and report on IC issues and events, both internally and externally. Reporting helps to foster a culture of patient safety and mitigate or eliminate infections.

Disseminating information about patient, resident, or staff risk, clearly, comprehensively, and appropriately to stakeholders is crucial to ensure effective care. There are many ways staff can communicate about infections, but typically internal reports are sent to organization leaders, committee members, and staff. External reports are sent to organizations such as the local or state health department, a national ministry of health, the National Healthcare Safety Network (NHSN), and consumers of health care. Communications about infections may include the following:

- Informing direct health care providers about the number and identity of patients and residents who have acquired infections on their units each month
- Discussing rates of infection and rates of compliance with organization policies for IC
- Providing information to modify physician, nursing, and other health care staff behavior for improved compliance with your organization's IC protocols.
- Empowering patients and residents to speak up when health care providers fail to properly follow hygiene protocols such as hand washing or cleaning injection ports and catheter hubs before accessing IV ports.

Establishing reporting systems: Reporting systems allow staff to phone, to e-mail, or to write reports about patients with infections. Individual infections are reviewed on an ongoing basis to look for serious individual infections and patterns, clusters, or outbreaks. If a cluster of infections is identified, IC professionals must act promptly to address the infection and to control the spread to other patients.

Chapter 8 | Evaluate and Improve Your Infection Prevention and Control Plan

Reporting systems are not as detailed or structured as surveillance (*see* Chapter 5), so underreporting can be an issue. To prevent underreporting, you'll need to do the following:

- Make it easy for staff to report potential infections.
- Avoid blaming or punishing staff members who report infection.
- Respond to all reports.

For a reporting system to work, staff needs to buy in to the idea that reporting infections, and other incidents, will improve the safety of patients and decrease infections. Giving feedback to staff who report potential infections will go a long way toward establishing trust and a commitment to your IC program and processes.

Reporting to external agencies: Collecting data and reporting it to external agencies, such as the local health department, the state or regional agencies, the CDC, or your country's ministry of health, is just as important to help identify infections, outbreaks, or new diseases before they get out of control. Public health agencies rely on organizations like yours to quickly report any unusual patterns or trends in infections. To do this, staff at your organization require an effective system in place to report externally. Make sure staff comply with local reporting laws, know what their reporting roles are, and recognize what outside authorities must be notified.

KEY CONCEPT

Drive Improvement

Performance improvement is vital to a successful IC program. As we've discussed, data and measurement are needed to assess the level of staff performance and determine whether improvement actions are necessary. But after you've gathered the data and assessed the strengths and weaknesses of your IC systems and processes, how do you take that information and improve the quality of IC in your physical environment?

in other words

Performance improvement
This term refers to the systematic process of detecting and analyzing performance problems, designing and developing interventions to address the problems, implementing the interventions, evaluating the results, and sustaining improvement.

165

Strategies for Implementing Change

You now have the data you need to start improving your IC program. But creating change, improving performance, and maintaining a system of continuous improvement requires more than numbers. To make successful changes, you'll need strong leadership, change agents and champions, and a proactive and collaborative approach. An emphasis on the culture of safety throughout your organization is the best way to ensure adherence to IC practices and continuous performance improvement.

Infection preventionist as improvement leader: If you're an infection preventionist or accreditation professional at your facility, driving improvement is one of your most important tasks. You, more than anyone else, have the ability to influence decisions regarding IC. To accomplish this you will need to work closely with staff and stakeholders, and guide, direct, and encourage corporate leaders to improve processes, set priorities, and allocate resources for preventing infection. In other words, your success and the success of the IC program depends on you influencing key people in your organization and establishing relationships to foster change.

- **Collaborate:** You will need to serve as champion for a safety culture in which prevention of HAIs is everyone's responsibility. You will coordinate multidisciplinary improvement efforts, navigate competing agendas and priorities, and encourage integration of prevention activities into the work of every department. Negotiation skills are vital.
- **Provide expertise and support:** When a multidisciplinary team is formed to prevent infections, you will take on a supportive role to provide your expertise and influence decisions. This is a difficult role, that relies on strong critical thinking skills, active engagement, and a willingness to provide constructive criticism and challenge leaders when necessary.
- **Communicate:** Communicating the value of IC to a diverse audience (verbally and on paper) is very important, as you will need to explain, influence, and demonstrate accountability and integrity to your organization. Effective communication requires you to be accurate, concise, and timely when presenting information. You must also take into account your audience:

Chapter 8 | Evaluate and Improve Your Infection Prevention and Control Plan

- – What is their background?
- – What is their knowledge of HAIs?
- – What are their informational needs?
- – What barriers might prevent communication?

Resources for improvement: You won't be able to implement change without the proper resources. Resources allocated to the IC plan will have a direct effect on the ability to protect patients and staff from infection. You need to solicit buy-in from leaders to obtain the resources you need.

Tips for Working Effectively with Leaders to Improve IC Activities

- Introduce yourself to the chief executive officer or president of the organization.
- Align departmental goals with the organization's strategic plan.
- Spend time with someone in the finance department to understand the costs of HAIs.
- Form collaborative relationships with directors and managers of clinical support departments, particularly those who directly affect IC activities such as nursing, laboratory, respiratory care, and staff or departments responsible for sterile processing.
- Establish close working relationships with staff responsible for managing the physical environment, purchasing, and materials management to promote easy exchange of ideas for process improvements related to IC.
- Provide regular updates to administration on the state of the IC activities in the organization, including infection rates.
- Attend all meetings and fulfill responsibilities associated with administrative appointments to committees and task forces.
- Negotiate for increased financial support or positions with data in hand on cost and opportunity savings associated with IC.
- Provide a brief, easy-to-read, and understandable annual report to administration on the infection rates in the facility or organization. Be sure to include cost savings associated with a decrease in infections, including opportunity costs.
- Establish a relationship based on mutual trust with the bedside caregivers and patient care managers because this is where the prevention and control activities take place.

> ### Key Joint Commission Standards on Performance Improvement
>
> **LD.03.05.01:** Leaders manage change to improve the performance of the [organization].
>
> **Element of Performance 1 for Standard LD.03.05.01**
>
> 1. The [organization] has a systematic approach to change and performance improvement.
>
> **LD.03.06.01:** Those who work in the [organization] are focused on improving safety and quality.
>
> **Elements of Performance 2–3 for Standard LD.03.06.01**
>
> 2. Leaders provide for a sufficient number and mix of individuals to support safe, quality care, treatment, and services. (*See also* IC.01.01.01, EP 3)
>   **Note:** *The number and mix of individuals is appropriate to the scope and complexity of the services offered.*
> 3. Those who work in the [organization] are competent to complete their assigned responsibilities.
>
> **IC.01.02.01:** [Organization] leaders allocate needed resources for the infection prevention and control program.
>
> **Elements of Performance 1–3 for Standard IC.01.02.01**
>
> 1. The [organization] provides access to information needed to support the infection prevention and control program. (*See also* IM.02.02.03, EP 2)
> 2. The [organization] provides laboratory resources when needed to support the infection prevention and control program.
> 3. The [organization] provides equipment and supplies to support the infection prevention and control program.

- Help remove barriers to change for managers who wish to look at new IC products and methods to prevent and control infections.

Integrating infection control goals into organizationwide strategic plans: Continuous improvement in quality and patient safety is stressed throughout the Joint Commission and JCI standards. When it comes to your IC program, JCI requires organizations to make certain that IC is given equal weight with other quality improvement measures, and that it is integrated with the organization's overall quality improvement and patient safety program. Doing so will lead to greater safety for patients and staff throughout your facility, as many of the practices in IC will also apply to other risks. PPE, for instance, is important but also applies to an overall plan to protect staff from injuries.

Chapter 8 | **Evaluate and Improve Your Infection Prevention and Control Plan**

Key Joint Commission International Standards on Performance Improvement

Standard PCI.10

The infection prevention and control process is integrated with the [organization's] overall program for quality improvement and patient safety, using measures that are epidemiologically important to the [organization].

Measurable Elements of Standard PCI.10

1. Infection prevention and control activities are integrated into the organization's quality improvement and patient safety program. (*Also see* GLD.4 and GLD.11, ME 1)
2. Monitoring data are collected and analyzed for the infection prevention and control activities and include epidemiologically important infections. (*Also see* PCI.6)
3. Monitoring data are used to evaluate and support improvements to the infection prevention and control program. (*Also see* QPS.8, ME 4)
4. Monitoring data are documented and reports of data analysis and recommendations are provided to leadership on a quarterly basis. (*Also see* GLD.4.1, ME 1)

Standard QPS.10

Improvement in quality and safety is achieved and sustained.

Measurable Elements of Standard QPS.10

1. Improvements in quality and patient safety are planned, tested, and implemented.
2. Data are available to demonstrate that improvements are effective and sustained. (*Also see* GLD.11, ME 3)
3. Policy changes necessary to plan, to carry out, and to sustain the improvement are made.
4. Successful improvements are documented.

Standard GLD.11

Department/service leaders improve quality and patient safety by participating in [organization-wide] improvement priorities and in monitoring and improving patient care specific to the department/service.

Measurable Elements of Standard GLD.11

1. Department/service leaders implement [organizationwide] quality measures that relate to the services provided by their department or service, including any contracted services for which they are responsible. (*Also see* PCI.10, ME 1 and FMS.10, ME 1)
2. Department/service leaders implement quality measures to reduce variation and improve processes within the department or service, including implementation of measures found in the Joint Commission International Library of Measures or other resources for well-defined, evidence-based clinical measures.
3. Department/service leaders select measures based on the need for improvement, and once improvement has been sustained, select a new measure. (*Also see* QPS.1, ME 3 and QPS.10, ME 2)
4. Department and service quality measurement and improvement activities are integrated into and supported by the quality management and coordination structure of the organization. (*Also see* QPS.10)

169

It's important to set goals for your organizationwide plan to minimize the transmission of infections. According to The Joint Commission and JCI, the goals should include the following:
- Address the prioritized risks.
- Limit unprotected exposure to pathogens.
- Limit transmission of infections associated with procedures.
- Limit transmission of infections associated with the use of medical equipment, devices, and supplies.
- Improve compliance with hand hygiene guidelines.

Your organization should base its goals, and the measurable objectives to meet those goals, on standards, best practices, and other recommendations related to the organization mission.

SMART Goals: The SMART Goal Methodology is one approach to creating practical objectives that can be written into strategic plans. Each letter in SMART refers to a different criterion for creating and judging objectives:
- Specific
- Measurable
- Action-oriented
- Realistic and relevant
- Timely or time-based

Goals and measurable objectives establish targets for performance improvement activities and allow you to evaluate progress and success or failure in these efforts. Table 8-2 on page 171 identifies key goals to consider for your IPC program as you integrate it into your organizationwide strategic plans.

TOOL OF THE TRADE

- Performance Improvement Tool Selection Matrix

Chapter 8 | **Evaluate and Improve Your Infection Prevention and Control Plan**

Table 8-2. Sample Goals and Objectives for the Infection Prevention and Control Program

Goal	Examples of Measurable Objectives
Reduce ventilator-associated pneumonias (VAPs) in the intensive care unit (ICU)	• Reduce VAP by equal to or greater than 50%, from 1.4/1,000 ventilator-days to 0.7/1,000 ventilator-days in the medical ICU (MICU), by June 2009 • Achieve zero VAPs for minimum of 3 months by January 2010 in the MICU • Assess daily whether the need for a ventilator is documented for 98% of ICU ventilated patients by January 2010
Decrease sharps injuries in employees	• Reduce needlestick injuries among direct care and support staff by at least 60% from the 2008 rate within first 6 months of 2009 • Reduce scalpel injuries in surgical staff by 80% from current rate with implementation of "pass zone" by July 2009
Increase immunizations in the organization	• Identify and immunize at least 90% of eligible patients with pneumococcal vaccine by December 2009 • Immunize 100% of eligible staff in organization with influenza vaccine within 6 months of initiating a mandatory flu vaccine program
Increase hand hygiene compliance	• Achieve at least 95% compliance with hand hygiene policy on at least 80% of nursing units by October 2009
Prevent transmission of infectious diseases in the organization	• Achieve at least 98% compliance with contact isolation policy for patients with methicillin-resistant *Staphylococcus aureus* (MRSA) and *Clostridium difficile* on all patient care units during 2010
Maintain consistent cleaning of reusable patient equipment in the ICUs	• Achieve at least 98% compliance with appropriate cleaning procedures for reusable direct care patient equipment during patient stay and at discharge in the MICU, surgical ICU, and neonatal ICU during 2010
Infection prevention and control staff notify staff about construction, renovation, or alteration in facility before beginning work	• Achieve equal to or greater than 95% notification to infection prevention and control staff before any construction, renovation, or alteration occurs in facility for all appropriate (per policy) construction projects by October 2009
Prepare for the response to an influx or risk of influx of infectious patients	• Meet equal to or greater than 90% of Hospital Emergency Incident Command System (HEICS) plan requirements related to infectious patients during at least three drills in 2010

Index

A

AAMI. *See* Association for the Advancement of Medical Instrumentation

Accreditation, 1, 2

    continuous compliance, 17, 19

    deemed status, 25

Accreditation professional, 24

Adenosine triphosphate (ATP) bioluminescence, 146

Aerosolizing water systems, 135

Agar slide plates, 146

Agency for Healthcare Research and Quality (AHRQ), 67

Airborne infection isolation, 56, 57–60

Airborne precautions, 84

Airflow, HVAC systems, 140–141, 162

American Society of Heating, Refrigerating and Air Conditioning Engineers (ASHRAE), 136, 139

Association for Professionals in Infection Control and Epidemiology (APIC), 111

Association for the Advancement of Medical Instrumentation (AAMI), standards, 119, 135

ATP bioluminescence, 146

B

Benchmarking, 63

Biohazards, 78, 128–129

Blood pressure machine, guidelines for cleaning, 122

C

Catheter-associated bloodstream infections (CABSIs), 47

Catheter-associated urinary tract infections (CAUTIs), 47, 99, 101

CAUTI Resource Page (website), 110

CDC Guideline for Hand Hygiene in Health-Care Settings, 89–90, 91

Center for Disease Control (CDC), 25, 70, 93

    CDC 2007 Guideline for Isolation Precautions: Preventing Transmission of Infections Agents in Healthcare, 73

    equipment and device reprocessing guidelines, 119

    evaluation of environmental cleaning, 144

    Guideline for Hand Hygiene in Health-Care Settings, 89–90, 91

    Guidelines for Disinfection and Sterilization in Healthcare Facilities, 119

    Guidelines for Environmental Infection Control in Health-Care Facilities, 119, 139, 162

Centers for Medicare & Medicaid Services (CMS), 25, 70

    equipment and device reprocessing guidelines, 119

    Hospital Infection Control Worksheet, 120

    Infection Control Worksheets for Ambulatory Surgical Centers and Hospitals, 120

Central line-associated bloodstream infections (CLABSIs), 42, 43, 47, 99, 101
CfCs. *See* Conditions for Coverage
CLABSI Resource Page (website), 110
CLABSIs. *See* Central line-associated bloodstream infections
Cleaners, 143
Cleaning
    environmental cleaning and disinfection, 142–147
        evaluating, 143–145
        surveillance, 145–147
    of medical equipment and devices
        about, 115
        blood pressure machine, 122
        guidelines and standards, 117–121
        monitors, 122
        personal protective equipment (PPE) for, 123
        pill crusher, 122
        radiology procedure table, 122
        risk mitigating strategies, 117–130
        risks associated with, 116–117
        tips for, 121–123
Clinical practice guidelines, 42
Clinicians, 24
CMS. *See* Centers for Medicare & Medicaid Services
Cold water systems, 135
Collaborating, 31–32
Communication, 31, 67–71
    during emergencies, 54–55
    with families of patients, 70
    influx of patients, 54–55
    preparedness, 54–55
    reporting to state Health Department, 70
    in risk assessment process, 44

A Compendium of Strategies to Prevent Healthcare-Associated Infections in Acute Care Hospitals, 111
Conditions for Coverage (CfCs), 25
Conditions of Participation (CoPs), 25
Construction. *See* Demolition, construction, or renovation
Contact precautions, 83
Cooling towers, 135
Coughing, 81, 82

D

Data
    benchmarking, 63
    collection, 63
    evaluating the infection control plan, 160–164
    reporting, 63–64
    sample hazard assessment, 48, 49
    surveillance, 48, 49
Data evaluation and analysis, 30, 162–163
Data mining, 36
Declination forms, vaccination, 88
Decontamination of medical equipment and devices, 115, 117–130
Deemed status, 25
Demolition, construction, or renovation
    educating staff, 148–149
    infection control during, 147–150, 162
    risk assessment, 147–148
    surveillance during, 149–150
Disinfectants, 143
Disinfection
    environmental cleaning and disinfection, 142–147
        evaluating, 143–145
        surveillance, 145–147

of medical equipment and devices
    about, 116
    areas requiring high-level disinfection, 125
    guidelines and standards, 117–121
    risk mitigating strategies, 117–130
    risks associated with, 116–117
    tips for, 123–125

Documentation, 14–16

Droplet precautions, 83–84

E

Education and training, 23–24, 50
    prevention of health care-associated infections (HAIs), 103–106
    of staff on influx procedures, 60–61

Electronic surveillance systems, 36

Elements of Performance (EPs), 16

Endoscope, reprocessing guidelines for, 119, 131

Environmental cleaning and disinfection, 142–147
    during demolition, construction, or renovation, 147–150
    evaluating, 143–145
    monitoring, 145–147
    resources, 150
    selecting cleaners and disinfectants, 143

Environmental services (EVS) director, 24

Environmental tours, during demolition, construction, or renovation, 149–150

Equipment. *See* Medical equipment and devices

Errors, reporting, 28

Ethylene Oxide Sterilization in Health Care Facilities: Safety and Effectiveness (AAMI ST41), 119

Evaluation
    of data, 30

of environmental cleaning and disinfection, 143–145

of infection control plan, 64–65, 151, 152–165
    collaboration, 159, 160
    data, 160–164
    evaluation report, 152–153, 157–159
    gap analysis, 158–159
    goals, 154–156
    Performance Improvement Matrix, 162
    process, 156
    reporting system for staff, 164–165
    revising the plan, 159–160
    risk assessment, 153–154
    sharing results, 157–159
    by tracers, 6, 8

Evaluation report
    components, 152–153
    gap analysis, 158–159
    sharing results, 157–159

Evidence-based practices
    health care-associated infections (HAIs), 109
    infection control plan guidelines, 42–43, 71–72

Executive leadership, 26, 50

External benchmarking, 63

Eye protection, 79

F

Face protection, 79

Facilities director or engineer, 24

Facilities management, 133–150

Facility demolition, renovation, and construction. *See* Demolition, renovation, or construction

Facility Guidelines Institute (FGI), 120–121, 136, 139, 147

175

Family, education for prevention of health care-associated infections (HAIs), 103, 104–106
FDA. See Food and Drug Administration
Filtration, hospitals, 140
Flexible and Semi-Rigid Endoscope Processing in Health Care Facilities (AAMI ST91), 119
Flu vaccinations, 86–89
Fluorescent markers, for surveillance, 146
Focused incidence surveillance, 47
Food and Drug Administration (FDA), 25
    medical equipment and devices reprocessing guidelines, 120
Frontline leadership, 27

G

Gloves, 79
Goals
    infection control plan, 48, 50–51, 154–156, 168, 170–171
    sample goals, 171
    SMART Goal Methodology, 170
Gowns, 79

H

HAIs. See Health care-associated infections
Hand hygiene, 36, 89–93
Harm, SAFER™ Matrix levels, 17
Hazardous waste, managing, 128–129
Head covers, 79
Health care-associated infections (HAIs), 43, 95–111
    catheter-associated urinary tract infections (CAUTIs), 47, 99, 101
    central line-associated bloodstream infections (CLABSIs), 42, 43, 47, 99, 101
    defined, 95
    education and training, 103–106
    evidence-based practices, 109
    medical equipment and device reprocessing, 113–131
        risk mitigating strategies, 117–130
    multidrug-resistant organisms (MDROs), 43, 96, 101
    reporting to state health department, 70
    resources, 110–111
    risk assessment, 101–103
    surgical site infections (SSIs), 47, 99, 100, 101
    surveillance, 107–108
Health Research & Educational Trust (HRET), 67
Healthcare Infection Control Practices Advisory Committee (HIPCAC), 71
Hospital and Critical Access Hospital Accreditation Survey Activity List, 4–5
Hospitals
    air change rates, 140–141
    air pressure relationships, 140, 162
    demolition, renovation, and construction, 147–150, 162
    environmental cleaning and disinfection, 142–147
    filtration, 140
    hand hygiene guidelines, 89–93
    Hospital and Critical Access Hospital Accreditation Survey Activity List, 4–5
    HVAC systems, 138–142
    influenza vaccinations, 86–89
    injection practices, 65–66, 73
    isolation, 56, 57–60
    medication management, 66
    personal protective equipment (PPE), 67, 79–80, 84, 123
    planning for influx of patients, 52–57
    room cleaning, 142–147
    special-care units, 140
    waterborne infectious agents, 134–138

See also Infection control plan; Infection prevention and control; Infectious disease transmission prevention; Patient safety

Hot water systems, 135

HRET. *See* Health Research & Educational Trust

HVAC systems, 138–142
- air change rates, 140–141
- guidelines, 139
- maintenance, 142
- pressure relationships, 140, 162

I

IC standards, 3

Immediate Threat to Health or Safety, 17

Immediate Threat to Life (ITL), 17, 18

Individual tracers, 8

Infection control plan
- allocation of resources, 22, 31, 62–63
- buy-in from leadership, 51
- communication, 54–55, 67–71
- components, 40–41
- demolition, renovation, and construction, 147–150, 162
- education in infection control, 50
- environment of care, 133–150
- environmental cleaning and disinfection, 142–147
- evaluation of, 64–65, 151, 152–165
- evidence-based guidelines, 42–43, 71–72
- executive and leadership support, 22–37, 50
- facilities management, 133–150
- facility demolition, renovation, and construction, 147–150, 162
- goals, 48, 50–51, 154–156, 168, 170–171
- hand hygiene guidelines, 89–93
- HVAC systems, 138–142
- implementing, 61–72
- improving, 151, 165–170
- infection expert training, 50
- multidisciplinary team involvement, 31, 32–33, 50
- orientation, 68–69
- outbreak preparedness, 50
- performance improvement, 50
- planning for influx of patients, 52–57
- preparedness, 50, 52–61
  - communication during emergencies, 54–55
  - for influx of infectious patients, 52–57
  - isolation, 56, 57–60
- public health reporting, 52
- resources, 93
- surveillance, 45–48
- utility systems, 134–142
- waterborne infectious agents, 134–138
- writing, 41–42

Infection control risk assessment (ICRA)
- defined, 148
- *See also* Risk assessment

Infection control system tracers, 8–14
- sample scenario: in an office-based surgery practice, 9–11
- sample scenario: influx of infectious patients in major metropolitan area, 11–13

Infection prevention and control (IC)
- accreditation or safety professional, 24
- allocating resources, 22, 31, 62–63
- clinicians, 24
- communicating and collaborating, 31–32, 54–55, 67–71
- data evaluation, 30
- demolition, renovation, and construction, 147–150, 162
- in environment of care, 133–150

environmental services (EVS) director, 24
establish partnerships, 34
evaluation of, 64–65, 151, 152–165
facilities director or engineer, 24
facilities management, 133–150
facility demolition, renovation, and construction, 147–150, 162
HVAC systems, 138–142
identifying IC individuals, 22
improving processes and systems, 28–30
integrating technologies, 34–37
international organizations for, 26
key staff, 23–24
leader's role, 22–37
measuring and analyzing performance data, 28–30
multidisciplinary team, 31, 32–33, 50
oversight group, 33
planning, 30, 39–61
preventing exposure, 76–84
preventing transmission, 75–94
prevention initiatives, 65–67
prioritizing patient safety, 21–37
regulatory organizations, 24–26
responsibility for, 22
safety culture, 27–28, 29
standards, 17, 19
waterborne infectious agents, 134–138
See also Infection control plan; Infectious disease transmission prevention; Safety precautions
Infection preventionist, 23–24, 50, 69, 127, 128, 166–167
Infectious disease
assessing risk, 44
Legionella, 134, 136–138
preparedness for influx of patients, 52–57
preventing transmission, 75–94
waterborne infectious agents, 134–138

See also Health care-associated infections; Infectious disease transmission prevention
Infectious disease transmission prevention, 75–94
airborne precautions, 84
contact precautions, 83
droplet precautions, 83–84
hand hygiene guidelines, 89–93
in health care staff, 85–94
influenza vaccinations, 86–89
personal protective equipment (PPE), 67, 79–80, 84, 123
resources, 93
respiratory hygiene, 81, 82
sharps, safe use, 77–78
transmission-based precautions, 81, 83–84
Influenza vaccinations, 86–89
Influx of patients, 52–54
accepting an influx, 55–56
communication, 54–55
isolation, 56, 57–60
tips for writing infection control plan, 55–57
Injection practices, 65–66, 73
Internal benchmarking, 63
International bodies
medical equipment maintenance, 128
reporting to ministries of health, 71
International Patient Safety Goals (IPSGs), 42, 96
International Patient Safety Goal (ISPG) 5, 3
International standards, 102
International survey process, 7
Isolation, 56, 57–60
Item reprocessing
defined, 114
See also Medical equipment and devices
ITL. *See* Immediate Threat to Life

178

Index

J

JCI. *See* Joint Commission International

Joint Commission, 24, 96
- accreditation process, 1, 2
- international survey process, 7
- standards, 17, 19, 118, 141, 151, 168
- survey process, 2–6
- tracer methodology, 6, 8–14

Joint Commission Infection Prevention and Control Portal, 110

Joint Commission International (JCI), 24, 96
- standards, 7, 19

L

Leaders/leadership, 22–37
- allocating resources, 22, 31, 62–63
- authority to intervene, 23
- backup authority, 23
- buy-in from, 51
- data evaluation, 30
- executive leadership, 26
- frontline leadership, 27
- improving processes and systems, 28–30
- infection preventionist, 23–24
- integrating technologies, 34–37
- measuring and analyzing performance data, 28–30
- multidisciplinary team, 31, 32–33, 50
- orientation, 68–69
- planning, 30, 39–61
- responsibilities, 22–23
- roles, 22–23, 26–32
- safety culture, 27–28, 29
- senior leadership, 26–27

Legionella, 134, 136–138

M

Masks, 79

MDROs. *See* Multidrug-resistant organisms

Medical equipment and devices
- planning for influx of patients, 56–57
- reprocessing, 113–131
  - categorization of items, 114–115
  - cleaning, 115–130
  - critical items, 114, 115
  - decontamination, 115
  - defined, 114
  - disinfection, 116–130
  - endoscope, 119, 130
  - guidelines and standards, 117–121
  - noncritical items, 115
  - risk assessment, 44
  - risk mitigating strategies, 117–130
  - risks associated with, 116–117
  - semicritical items, 114, 115
  - single-use devices (SUDs), 130
  - sterilization, 116–130
  - storage and disposal, 44, 129
- storage and disposal, 44, 129

Medication management, 66

Mock tracers, 14

Monitoring. *See* Surveillance

Monitors, guidelines for cleaning, 122

Multidisciplinary team, 31, 32–33, 50

Multidrug-resistant organisms (MDROs), 43, 96, 101

N

National Healthcare Safety Network (NHSN), 70

National Institute for Occupational Safety and Health (NIOSH), 25

National Patient Safety Goals® (NPSGs), 42
    National Patient Safety Goal 7, 3, 43, 96–98
Needlesticks, 77
NHSN. See National Healthcare Safety Network
NIOSH. See National Institute for Occupational Safety and Health

O

Occupational Safety and Health Administration (OSHA), 25, 136, 138
Orientation, 68–69
OSHA. See Occupational Safety and Health Administration
Outbreak preparedness, 50
Outcome monitoring, 47
Oversight group, 33

P

Partnerships, 34
Patient safety, 21–37
    airborne precautions, 84
    contact precautions, 83
    droplet precautions, 83–84
    during demolition, renovation, or construction, 149
    education for prevention of health care–associated infections (HAIs), 103, 104–106
    establish partnerships, 34
    hand hygiene guidelines, 89–93
    influenza vaccinations, 86–89
    integrating technologies, 34–37
    key staff, 23–24
    multidisciplinary teams, 31, 32–33, 50
    regulatory organizations, 24–26
    safety culture, 27–28, 29
    sentinel event, 31
    See also Infection control plan; Infection prevention and control; Leaders/leadership
PCI standards, 3, 102, 118, 130
Performance data, measuring and analyzing, 28–30
Performance Improvement Matrix, 162
Personal protective equipment (PPE), 67, 74, 79–80, 123
Pill crusher, guidelines for cleaning, 122
Planning, 30, 39–61
    communication, 31, 67–71
    evidence-based guidelines, 42–43, 71–72
    facility demolition, renovation, and construction, 147–150, 162
    goals, establishing, 48, 50–51, 168
    preparedness, 50, 52–61
    risk assessment for, 41, 43–48
    surveillance, 45–48
    writing the IC plan, 41–42
Point-of-care testing (POCT), 35–36
PPE. See Personal protective equipment
Precleaning, 125, 130
Preparedness, 50, 52–61
    communication during emergencies, 54–55
    for influx of infectious patients, 52–54
Prevalence surveillance, 47–48
Prevention. See Infection prevention and control; Safety precautions
Problem-oriented surveillance, 47
Process monitoring, 46–47
Pseudomonas aeruginosa, 134, 138

R

Radiology procedure table, guidelines for cleaning, 122
Real-time location system (RTLS) technology, 36
Regulatory organizations, 24–26

Index

Renovation. *See* Demolition, construction, or renovation

Repair, infection control during, 147–150

Respirators, 79

Respiratory hygiene, 81, 82

Risk assessment
  for CAUTIs, 101
  for CLABSIs, 101
  communicating responsibilities, 44
  defined, 101, 148
  for demolition , construction, or renovation, 147–148
  equipment and waste, 44
  evaluation of infection control plan, 153–154
  health care-associated infections (HAIs), 101–103
  of infectious disease, 44
  for MDROs, 101
  medical equipment and device reprocessing, 44
  for planning, 41, 43–48
  process, 44–45
  scoring matrix, 49
  for SSIs, 101

Risk assessments, for infection prevention: questions, 103

Room cleaning, 142–147

RTLS technology. *See* Real-time location system (RTLS) technology

S

Safe injection practices, 65–66, 73

SAFER™ Matrix, 16–19

Safety culture, 27–28, 29

Safety precautions, 76–94
  personal protective equipment (PPE), 67, 79–80, 84, 123

preventing exposure to infection, 76–84
  preventing infection transmission, 75–94
  respiratory hygiene, 81, 82
  sharps, 77–78
  standard precautions, 76–77

Safety professional, 24

Scope, SAFER™ Matrix levels, 17

Senior leadership, 26–27

Sentinel event, 31

Sharps, 77–78

SHEA. *See* Society for Healthcare Epidemiology of America

Shoe covers, 79

Single-use devices (SUDs), reprocessing, 130

SMART Goal Methodology, 170

Sneezing, 81

Society for Healthcare Epidemiology of America (SHEA), 111

Spaulding classification, 114

Special-care units, 140

SSIs. *See* Surgical site infections

Staff
  accreditation or safety professional, 24
  clinicians, 24
  education for prevention of health care-associated infections (HAIs), 103–104
  education on influx procedures, 60–61
  environmental services (EVS) director, 24
  facilities director or engineer, 24
  infection preventionist, 23–24
  infectious disease transmission prevention, 85–94
  influenza vaccinations, 86–89
  leaders' roles, 22–23
  See also Leaders/leadership

State Health Department, reporting to, 70

Sterilization of medical equipment and devices
  about, 116
  guidelines and standards, 117–121

181

maintenance and testing of sterilizers, 127–128
monitoring, 127
precleaning, 125, 130
procedures for, 126
risk mitigating strategies, 117–130
risks associated with, 116–117
tips for, 125–128
transporting items for reprocessing, 126
Sterilizers, maintenance and testing, 127–128
Storage and disposal, medical equipment and device reprocessing, 44, 129
SUDs. See Single-use devices
Surgical site infections (SSIs), 47, 99, 100, 101
Surveillance
    agar slide plates, 146
    ATP bioluminescence, 146
    of cleaning and disinfection methods, 145–147
    data, 48, 49
    defined, 45
    during demolition, construction, or renovation, 149–150
    fluorescent markers, 146
    focused incidence surveillance, 47
    infection control plan, 45–48
    outcome monitoring, 47
    prevalence surveillance, 47–48
    prevention of health care-associated infections (HAIs), 107–108
    problem-oriented surveillance, 47
    process monitoring, 46–47
    sterilization of medical equipment and devices, 127
    swab cultures, 145–146
    targeted surveillance, 47
    types, 46–48
Survey Analysis for Evaluating Risk™ Matrix. See SAFER™ Matrix
Surveys, 2–6
    as collaborative process, 13–14
    documentation, 14–16
    frequency of, 6
    Hospital and Critical Access Hospital Accreditation Survey Activity List, 4–5
    sample survey agenda, 3–4
    See also SAFER™ Matrix
Swab cultures, 145–146
System tracers, 8

T

Targeted Solutions Tool® (TST®), 92
Targeted surveillance, 47
Technology
    choosing, 36–37
    integrating, 34
    types
        data mining, 36
        electronic surveillance systems, 36
        hand hygiene monitoring, 36
        information technology (IT)-based surveillance, 36
        point-of-care testing (POCT), 35–36
        real-time location system (RTLS) technology, 36
Tracers, 6, 8–14
    evaluation and assistance by, 6, 8
    individual tracers, 8
    infection control system tracers, 8–14
        sample scenario: in an office-based surgery practice, 9–11
        sample scenario: influx of infectious patients in major metropolitan area, 11–13
    mock tracers, 14
    system tracers, 8
Training. See Education and training

Index

U

Unsafe injection practices, 65–66, 73

V

Vaccinations, 86–89
Ventilator-associated events (VAEs), 47

W

Water distribution systems, 134–136
Water supply
    Legionella contamination, 134, 136–138
    water quality testing, 162
Waterborne infectious agents, 134–138
World Health Organization (WHO), 110–111
    Guidelines on Hand Hygiene in Health Care, 90
    medical equipment and devices reprocessing guidelines, 121